Out of the Box—Skills for Developing Your Own Career Path

Mark D. Hansen, P.E., CPE, CSP

AMERICAN SOCIETY OF SAFETY ENGINEERS ❖❖ Des Plaines, Illinois

Out of the Box—Skills for Developing Your Own Career Path

Library of Congress Cataloging-In-Publication Data

Hansen, Mark D.
    Out of the box : skills for developing your own career path / Mark D. Hansen.
      p. cm.
    Includes bibliographical references.
    ISBN 1-885581-38-6
    1. Career development. I. Title

    HF5381 .H1363 2002
    650.14--dc21   2002018943

Project Editor: Charles T. Coffin
Copy Editor: Cathy Lombardi
Text Design, Composition, and Layout: Cathy Lombardi
Cover Design: Publication Design, Inc.
Managing Editor: Michael F. Burditt

07 06 05 04   6 5 4 3

Printed in the United States of America

Table of Contents

Foreword

With hundreds of books on career building available today, why would anyone even consider writing another one? What more could be said? From a core technical point of view, this may very well be the case. But from a management point of view, safety-related information is scarce. There is no college course that teaches you how to manage your career in the safety, health, and environmental fields. This course is taught daily in the school of hard knocks—the business world.

That is the impetus for writing this book. The goal was to answer several probing questions. Questions like, **what do you do when** . . . you are about to get laid off? . . . you have to discipline or fire an employee? . . . your company is about to merge with another company and your job may be in question? Or, **how do you** . . . get to the corner office? . . . negotiate your salary? . . . convince management of the fiduciary efficiency of safety? . . . lead? . . . follow? . . . run effective meetings?

When these questions arise, they require timely responses. A poorly crafted answer could put your job on the line. This book will help you prepare for those career landmines. Hopefully, it will provide tried and true methods on how to manage, lead, follow, and survive during trying times.

No one can start from humble beginnings as a young professional from a small town and arrive at a corporate safety management position in one of the largest cities in the country, merely by good fortune, luck, or coincidence. That can only be accomplished through prudent planning; in particular, the judicious development and monitoring of a five-year plan.

Five-year plans are quite ubiquitous; everyone has one and no one has one. As a young safety engineer at Ford Aerospace in 1988, I survived unprecedented layoffs at that company. It was not an easy time. Able professionals lost their jobs. Some who should have been laid off were not. Some were retained because they knew the right people. It was not fair. But life, as we all know, is not always fair. As a result of this experience, I decided to change career fields. I thought, "This shouldn't be too hard. After all, safety is safety no matter what you are applying it to. Right?" **Wrong!** I discovered very quickly the parochial nature of industry.

My first realization came while working with a company that was bidding on a safety contract at NASA. The contract was awarded to a competitor and the reason given was that "NASA safety was *very different* from Air Force safety." Huh?! I had worked both and found only subtle differences. Slap me in the face! After only a few years in industry, I had been pigeon-holed in a perceived arcane and small category of safety called "system safety." I asked myself a series of questions, "If NASA has this predisposition, what about the rest of industry? Am I stuck here for the duration of my career, whether I like it or not? Do I have to go back to school to diversify and break the image?" It was at this point that I assembled a five-year plan. I worked that plan to transition out of aerospace into oil and gas.

So how does one transition from a stereotyped career? You do several things. First, find local universities where you can teach safety-related courses, safety engineering, safety management, human factors and ergonomics. As an instructor with a master's degree, you are a welcome source of cheap labor. In several cases, I was able to teach graduate-level courses. Not only were students being educated, but I found teaching quite enjoyable. It also refreshed everything I had learned in college and diversified my resume. I thought it might offer contact with potential employers, perhaps even some consulting opportunities. All of this and more happened.

In any industry you only apply a slice of what you know to what you are doing. Teaching allowed me to brush up on all that I had learned. Listing the courses I taught diversified my resume, adding general safety rather than only system safety. I made contacts with company representatives that needed specific assistance in safety and ergonomics. Consulting provided me work on the side and further diversified my resume. My plan began to work.

I knew that I could not transition directly from aerospace to oil and gas, so I had to find at least one and possibly several transition midpoints. The first one was a small company that split its activities between Department of Energy (DOE) business and commercial business. I was hired as the Manager of Environmental Safety & Health. Good title. No hint of aerospace, even though the company still did some of that work. Transition midpoint one was now complete. The plan was to stay in this position for two to three years. My tenure there lasted about a year and a half; an opportunity came along that provided a step closer to my goal, and I could not pass it up.

As a long-term and active member of the American Society of Safety Engineers (ASSE), I was able to network my way through the transition. Although I lived in Colorado, I had contacts throughout the United States. While attending an American Petroleum Institute (API) conference, I met a colleague and went to a local section and chapter meeting with him. A few months later, he called me regarding an opening at a chemical processing company in Texas. I promptly sanitized my resume of the term "System Safety." An interview was actually granted. I didn't think I would get an offer, but I did. I took the job. Transition midpoint two was now complete.

Several references from consultants in my ASSE network helped me to get that job. I was enamored by the glamour and breadth of a consultant's work. Several years later I bit at the carrot, thinking it would be a great career. This was probably my only mistake, but it later turned out to be a blessing. You have to be cut out for consulting. Discovering it was not my cup of tea, I began the search for another job. This would complete the transition. Fortunately, a number of opportunities arose. With proven industry experience, I was now a commodity.

I landed the job I had envisioned seven years earlier—corporate safety manager in an oil and gas company. Transition complete. The position was offered because of my consulting and processing-plant experience. So the consulting experience actually helped to qualify me for the job. None of this would have happened without prudent planning.

End of story, right? Happy ending, right? Stay here for the duration of my career, right? Wishful thinking. Two years after landing the job of my dreams, on April 1, 1998 (no joke), the company was swallowed up by a larger, cash-rich oil company looking for a smaller independent to purchase. It was called a merger, but for all intents and purposes, it was a buyout. All that security and enjoyment went poof—right in front of my eyes! Surviving an acquisition became the next strategy to develop. Oddly, the strategy in the final analysis was to convince the company to sever me. Another company with a similar culture approached me with a position that afforded more responsibility.

Along the way, I had to learn how to do things like negotiate my salary, play company politics, survive layoffs, discover many ways to find jobs, pick the right company, figure out how to get ahead without stepping on people, bring good talent with me, and lead, follow, and manage what I did. I also had to grow and mature. I grew from the stereotypical arrogant engineer (with an attitude of "I'm right, you're stupid") to a humble professional

("That's interesting, have you also considered … ?") This was not easy. And the journey is not yet over.

What is assembled in these pages are answers to the probing questions, "What do I do when …?" and, "How do I … ?" when it comes to managing your safety career. Hopefully, when you face one of these questions, this book can help you make the right decision or at least point you in the right direction. Perhaps you can learn from my experience and avoid some of my mistakes. Or, perhaps you will break new ground, only using this book as a starting point. Whichever it is, I hope it helps you successfully manage your safety career.

Acknowledgments

Although many hours and much blood, sweat, and tears went into writing this book, none of it was achieved alone. Many thanks go my wife, Kathryn, who supported me through the bad times and celebrated with me through the good times. Also, many thanks go to my daughter, Hannah, who has unknowingly given me the strength to push forward as a father, which in return, I feel, has made me a better professional. I also want to acknowledge my Pastor, Ron Hindt, who teaches me and encourages me to be a man of integrity. Clearly, I would not have been able to get this far in life without God and my family walking with me and gently guiding me to this place in my career.

Many of the things I learned in my career have been from bad examples and from observing characteristics that I wanted to avoid emulating. But these were far outweighed by the positive attributes I learned from exceptional people. Our profession is replete with such individuals. The list of those whom I learned positive attributes from is long and distinguished. I hesitate to mention a few, fearing I might leave out someone deserving. Having said that, here is the short list: Margaret Carroll, who through many years of mentoring, provided me with much of the initial steam and political savvy in my career. George and Theo Huber, who gave me inspiration from what they endured before there were any regulations and legislation for us to ensure safe workplaces. James Kohn, whose integrity and dedication to safety is unparalleled in anyone else I have known. Ray Rigby, who provided me with the upper-management view of business. And Frank Perry, who gave me the humble servant-leader profile from which to successfully manage people. This list would not be complete without also mentioning the many people I have had the pleasure of working with at the headquarters of the American Society of Safety Engineers in Des Plaines, Illinois.

Much of what I have learned throughout my career has come from the many professionals with whom I have come in contact. Our profession is one of sharing information to prevent people from getting injured in the workplace. The safety professionals I have met along my journey have all freely shared information to this end. What a great profession we belong to!

For those of us who are safety professionals, safety is not just a job, or a career, but a *passion* and a *lifestyle*. That is why we love it so much.

Mark Hansen

Getting to the Corner Office

To Get Ahead Quicker, Build Your Visibility

Almost everyone knows that working hard at your job isn't enough to keep your professional star rising. Just as important to advancing your career is being visible both in and outside of your company. You may think that keeping your nose to the grindstone is the best way to get ahead—that if you work hard enough, someone is bound to notice and reward you.

But this isn't the best way to get ahead. A better way to gain visibility is to make internal and external contacts and to seek out developmental assignments at your company. High visibility actually is the end-product of being a good networker. This means doing those things that help you become known as an effective, take-charge person to people who might remember you when opportunities develop later.

But if you have more work than ever on your professional plate, how can you find the time to make this happen? And what specifically should you do?

Be careful, there is a right and wrong way to attract attention. In fact, you should never be perceived as doing something specifically to gain exposure. For instance, sending a note to senior management touting a recent achievement or making a speech because you enjoy the attention are no-nos. There's nothing worse than tooting your own horn unnecessarily. No one has time for that. Plus, it is far more credible if someone else mentions your accomplishments, because you have a vested interest in things you say about yourself.

Here are some reasonable and effective ways to build visibility for yourself without being seen as an opportunist:

1. **Start on your home turf.** Gaining internal visibility is a necessity, particularly if you work for a large company where it's hard to meet people in geographically dispersed business units. Volunteer for cross-disciplinary task forces where you can learn about other functions. If you're asked to head a committee, look outside the usual channels when choosing other members and select people you specifically want to meet.

Another good, though often overlooked, option: Volunteer to be a trainer for internal courses or recruitment sessions. For example, volunteer to give a thirty-minute presentation to all employees on ergonomics. Companies usually require all employees, including upper management and the president, to attend such presentations. Wow! What exposure!

2. **Don't be insular.** Become known on the outside. In some professions external recognition is more important than internal acclaim, and joining professional societies such as the American Society of Safety Engineers (ASSE) and the American Industrial Hygiene Association (AIHA) is essential to your career. Most fields have one or more established profes-

sional associations that you can investigate. But don't merely send in your dues and read the newsletter. You'll gain the greatest benefit by becoming an active participant.

Are you one of those silent members? Make it a priority in your career to be a participant rather than an observer in your professional societies.

Join professional organizations whose work is valued by your employer, then strive to take a leadership role that will reflect positively on your employer. This provides your employer with important visibility. The president of a small chemical company would take reprints of the safety director's computer column with him when he met with potential customers and brag about how good their safety program was. He would also make sure that they saw the by-line, stating the safety director's volunteer position on the Board of Directors of ASSE. This helped the company attract business and receive much of the funding it asked for.

Taking part in a professional group provides many benefits, from staying abreast of developments in your industry to being noticed by company recruiters and headhunters who often join as associate members and attend functions to meet prospective candidates. You never know who is going to notice you.

Those who are not active in their professional societies are out of the loop when it comes to trade-related information. They may not be apprised of their smaller competitors and what they are doing. If you are involved, you will be able to keep abreast of recent happenings at competing firms as well as activities at the Occupational Safety and Health Administration (OSHA), National Institute of Safety and Health (NIOSH), International Organization for Standardization (ISO), and other agencies that may affect safety and your profession.

3. **Take on and fix an albatross for the company.** There's no
    better way to gain visibility than by taking on an unpopular,
    high-risk assignment and succeeding at it. You can literally
    build a career on high-risk tasks others have failed to complete.
    If you manage to tame those albatrosses, they will boost
    your career.

At Ford Aerospace, a safety professional was assigned as the
Principal Investigator after two of his predecessors had been unsuccessful moving a project forward. After implementing some
key strategies, the ranking of that project rose from eleventh to
second of twelve. The project was completed under budget and
on schedule and received funding from the parent Ford Motor
Company. What a coup! Handling these kinds of roles gives you
battle scars that can mark you for bigger and better things. In
many cases, the payoff is only evident *after* the job is finished.

4. **Step outside of your comfort zone.** Taking on new func-
    tional roles grabs the attention of upper management. Never
    turn down new functional assignments, even if they aren't
    in your area of specialty. Never be afraid to take on reliabil-
    ity, maintainability, security, and other disciplines that will
    show your diversity. The result will be increased visibility.

5. **Limit yourself.** You can't do everything. Neither should you
    try. Participate in an activity because you find it personally
    or professionally stimulating. Then your natural enthusiasm
    for your work will impress others. If you spend an undue
    amount of time seeking visibility by joining every single proj-
    ect team and task force, you'll be everywhere, and you won't
    be perceived as sincere. Remember, you can either do a few
    things well or many things poorly.

6. **Be very good at what you do.** At your core, you should al-
    ways be known as someone who is highly effective. Other-

wise, no amount of attention-getting activity will help you. Simply participating in task forces isn't what gets you promoted. At the end of the day, visibility can give you an assist, but it's the quality of the job you do that will get you ahead.

These are only some of the things that will help you get ahead and build your visibility. Choose a few at a time to work on. Once you feel that you have plateaued, work on a few others. As you grow in your career, more ways to build your visibility will present themselves. Taking on these challenges is the best preparation for dealing with the changes you will undoubtedly face in the workplace.

Change Happens

Things change every day. Newspapers report on changes, David Bowie sings about it, and each and every day, to some degree, we must all deal with change in both our personal and professional lives. Change is that omnipresent phenomenon that frequently undermines whatever sense of well-being we attempt to create for ourselves.

Sometimes, change is welcome. Every one of us has pursued it at one point or another in our lives, whether it was seeking a job change, going back to school, or making a New Year's resolution. Usually, however, change is a threatening proposition. As creatures of habit, we tend to like the status quo, even if it is not good for us. Remember the title of the play of years ago, *Been Down So Long Looks Like Up to Me*? Sometimes a routine can become so comfortable, so reassuring, that we avoid facing the fact that we are on the verge of stagnation.

Facing change in a system or program can be especially confusing. Although we like to think of ourselves as free-spirited individuals, most of us appreciate the stability that rules and other standards provide. We rely on calendars, schedules, and Day-Timers to *plan* our day-to-day lives. Whether it's an annual review of a program or a five-year submittal of a program to a government agency, we rely heavily on schedules. If you don't believe me, just listen to the complaints a simple change of one hour for daylight savings time engenders. Even this small change elicits much discussion.

The alternative to change, obviously, is that everything remains the same, day-in and day-out. On and on and on and on, every day, the same things. How boring! Even if you could wield such power, would you really want to go through life like some automated robot at Disney World?

Being a safety professional means, in part, that you not only accept change but actually are an agent for change in many cases. Companies hire us, not because everything is "coming up roses," but because they need help. People may be getting hurt or sick, and they want to reverse that trend. *Change* is what we must bring to companies that want to keep employees healthy.

We've all heard comments like "How can companies so large have such a small incident rate? Some of them are either zero or near zero! They have to be lying or not reporting! There's no way they can do that. We get finger cuts not monthly, not weekly, but daily! I just don't believe it! How can they do it when we can't?"

Well, the answer is you can! But it isn't easy! It takes work, commitment by safety and management, knowledge of how to effect change, and the discipline to stick with it through both the peaks and valleys of incident rates. You have to press on when things are bad and get as much backing as you can when things are good. Get the funding when it is clear that you need new equipment and personnel, and get even more funding when you are riding the high of successes and low incident rates.

How It Can Be Done

First, remove as many hazards as possible through—you guessed it—engineering design. Remember the inherently safe statement by Trevor Kletz, "It can't hurt you if it doesn't exist." Assess the situation from an engineering standpoint. Identify engineering controls through design that would eliminate the hazards presented or mitigate them to an acceptable level. Granted, it is difficult to remove all hazards, so identify the significant hazards and mitigate those. Accomplish this using a vehicle that involves the employees, like a Safety Task Force. Avoid the word "committee," since it implies just sitting around and talking.

When the task force is well under way, formulate an overall strategy. Successful safety programs are contingent on successful planning. Take as much time and effort as you need during the formative stages of this process. To carry out the plan, allow a time frame of two to five years. Next, set a goal that is achievable, such as an incident rate of 2.5 over two years.

The final step is to implement the plan. Build a team that can assist you in that implementation: Make sure you include your boss, emergency response, field safety, and industrial hygiene. The goals of this team could be something like the following:

+ **Increased Safety Personnel Presence in the Plant.** This is the equivalent of management by walking around.
+ **Routine Auditing of Safety Procedures Throughout the Plant.** When confined-space work is going on, stop by and chat with those involved and see that they are doing things right and whether improvements can be made.
+ **Enforcement of Policies and Procedures Followed by Disciplinary Action Where Required.** Yes, the "D" word. *Discipline* is a key to successful program implementation— no matter what else anyone tells you. If you elect to imple-

ment a behavior-based safety program, remember, it is only one piece of the overall picture.

+ **Safety Program Implementation.** Find out what programs have already been written and what programs need to be written, and then write them.

+ *(Optional)* **Process Safety Management (PSM) Program Implementation.** Is the site a PSM site? If so, develop and implement a PSM program if one is not already in place. If your site is not a PSM site, consider implementing the philosophy of PSM. PSM provides an excellent management system to implement safety. Also, the Volunteer Protection Program (VPP) is a potential goal.

+ **Emergency Response Team (ERT) Involvement.** If there is no ERT, set one up immediately. Consider training employees as Emergency Care Attendants (ECAs) or Emergency Medical Technicians (EMTs). Train the ERT on prehospital medical care, rescue, and HAZMAT.

+ **Increase in Safety Training Meeting Attendance.** Make meetings enjoyable as well as informative. Please, please don't read Material Safety Data Sheets (MSDS) for the required Hazard Communication and Right-to-Know training. Snooze!

+ **Employee Safety Awareness Through Safety Newsletters.** Get the word out to everybody through newsletters—this includes management as well as employees. They let everyone know what you are doing and when you are doing it.

+ **Prompt Mitigation of Corrective Actions Following Incident Investigations.** After an incident, literally jump on the corrective actions and remove the potential hazards from the workplace. Don't just point the finger at employees and say, "Don't do that."

+ **Progress of a Safety Task Force.** Advertise the task force successes and make ongoing improvements in the facility.

+ **Flame Retardant Clothing (FRC)/Uniform Program Implementation.** Examine such a program closely and implement one that suits the facility and the industry.
+ **Workers' Compensation Control.** Implement measures for Workers' Compensation cost control that get employees back to work as soon as they can return to work and minimize potential misuse and abuse by employees.
+ **Safety Orientation.** Use videos and hands-on instruction, mixing it up to make this activity less boring. Remember to give an exam afterwards!

Introducing options like these can effect a measured culture change at your facility. Yes, it can be done, but it takes hard work, cooperation, involvement by many, and patience. In a year or so you, too, can turn accidents while building that aircraft carrier from a high rate to a low rate—and perhaps approach, or even attain, that ever-elusive goal of zero.

In fact, you might discover that change is one of the secrets to success and getting things done. Remember, stagnation can be a company albatross, and incremental change is like eating that albatross, one bite at a time.

Secrets for Success and Getting Things Done

Do you ever feel that you are always wasting time? Do you feel that the more hurried you become, the more behind you get? In this information and computer-driven world, our list of things to do can seem bottomless. Through the years I have developed some strategies to help better manage my time and create more balance in my life. Some of these things are:

1. **Concentrate.** When you concentrate on a task, you focus your attention on it and that, in turn, focuses your energy. It's hard

to be distracted when you're truly concentrating. When you are very busy, don't immediately answer a phone call unless you know it is an emergency. Implement the consultant's Dr. Pepper approach to answering calls: Check your messages at 10–2–4. Don't return all calls. Selectively answer the business calls at times when you know you will be leaving a message, and leave a detailed message so you will not need to make a return phone call. This allows more time to concentrate and focus on activities that require your immediate attention.

2. **Honor your personal time clock.** Are you a morning person who jumps out of bed at 5 A.M. rarin' to go? Or are you a nighttime person who can't function before 10 A.M. and hits his or her stride at 2 P.M.? If you're a morning person, schedule presentations and make important decisions early in the morning while you're in your prime. If you're a nighttime person, schedule important activities in the afternoon or early evening. If you have an early morning meeting, prepare everything you need the night before, and eat a high-protein breakfast.

   If you don't honor your time clock, you will find that you will run out of gas in the middle of the week without time to recharge your batteries. It would not reflect well on you if this occurred in the middle of a big meeting with the plant manager or the president of the company.

3. **Motivate yourself and others to take action.** People are either motivated toward a goal or away from the consequences of not acting. People are motivated for a wide variety of reasons. When you understand other people's motivational styles, you can communicate goals and performance requirements so that people respond in the way you want them to.

4. **Know when to act.** Don't respond to everything that comes across your desk. Ask three questions about each activity: Does the activity have value? Does the activity have a deadline? Is the activity urgent or does it have a deadline of less than one week away?

   When you ask the question, "Does the activity have value?" you are analyzing whether you even need to do it at all. You shouldn't do things just because you have always done them. If you decide the activity has no real value, simply don't do it anymore.

   Secondly, make sure that you are improving the process rather than taking away from the process. Try to think outside the box to determine if there is a better way to do it. If there is, pursue doing it the new way rather than the old way. If you determine you cannot add value to a process, don't touch it.

   When you ask the question, "Does the activity have a deadline?" you want to know when you should schedule the activity—today, tomorrow, the end of the week, two weeks from now, next month, next quarter, or next year. Just because it came across your desk today doesn't mean it has to be done today. If you have time, you'll do it. But if other things more important are pending, those items take priority. If it is due more than two weeks away, you can put it on your near-term calendar.

   When you ask the question, "Is the activity urgent or does it have a deadline of less than one week away?" you ascertain its immediacy. If it is within the two-week window, you can schedule it on your short-term calendar.

5. **Work smarter every day.** Try to learn something every day. I once heard something while attending a leadership confer-

ence that stuck with me over the years. I overheard someone say, "I'm only forty-one years old, but I read at the forty-three-year-old level." This person is learning every day. That is the kind of person you want to be.

Also, try to improve your communication skills every day. Fifty percent of all communications fail. Try to repeat yourself whenever necessary, and try to make your first communication clear and within the attention span of the hearer.

Stop Wasting Time!

According to Alec MacKenzie in *The Time Trap: The Classic Book on Time Management* (3rd ed.), here are the twenty biggest time-wasters affecting workers today:

+ Telephone interruptions
+ Inadequate planning
+ Drop-in visitors
+ Lack of self-discipline
+ Paperwork
+ Meetings
+ Procrastination
+ Socializing
+ Poor communication
+ Travel
+ Incomplete information
+ Personal disorganization
+ Attempting too much
+ Management by crisis
+ Ineffective delegation
+ Inability to say "no"
+ Confused responsibility or authority
+ Inadequate staff

+ Leaving tasks unfinished
+ Inadequate controls and progress reports

Paperwork: Conquering the In-Basket

The in-basket is an essential tool to help you get your scattered papers under control. Here are some exercises to help you make the most of it.

+ Sort through the papers in your in-basket twice a day.
+ Assign each paper a proper location.
+ Put papers relating to a project you are currently working on in a project file.
+ Create a reading file for all periodicals and newsletters.
+ Put notes or e-mails from friends in your personal file.
+ Put any item you need to discuss with a client in a file with that person's name on it.
+ Throw away early drafts of proposals and client letters.
+ Scan and save only the material that you are likely to read in depth.
+ When your reading file is full, sort the oldest portion and ask, "How likely am I to read or refer to this in the near future?" Then respond accordingly.
+ Put things away quickly. Once you set it aside "just for a minute," the piles will begin to take over.

Take Charge of Your Career to Avoid Unpleasant Surprises

Will this be the year you get the ax? The truth is, in today's job climate we're all at risk of losing our jobs. In case you've just pulled your head out of a hole in the ground, the covenant between employers and employees is gone, and job security has vanished. Companies renowned for their loyalty to dedicated employees are, alas, practically nonexistent. Your next best career move may be to leave your company.

The watchphrase for the new millennium is simple: Your job is temporary, your career path is uncharted, and the future of the company you work for is unclear. Corporate flowcharts have been flattened, vertical promotions are down, and lateral reassignments are the rage. The technology curve is down to eighteen months. At a competitive company, virtually every computer, software program, communication system, and business process is less than two years old. Blink, and—oops—you're out or antiquated.

What do these changes mean for safety professionals? You'd better be prepared for any event. Pack your parachute and strap it on because you never know when you'll need it. We're all in a career airplane, standing much too near an open hatch. Complacency is dangerous and can spell the end of any career. As a youngster, I was a Boy Scout, and the Scouts' motto still rings true today: Be Prepared.

Take Charge

If you think this might be your year to get the ax, don't live in denial. Instead of trying to avoid the new business world, embrace it. You have to get up every morning and take every day as a gift. There are so many people who think their last promotion was some kind of reward. They come to the office, drink coffee, read the *Wall Street Journal*, write a couple of e-mails, and then go to lunch. They have what I call the "I've earned it" mentality, and they forget that they've got to earn their job *every day*. It's a globally competitive marketplace out there, and we have to face a lot of competitors to fight for our jobs.

We all know someone who was fired or laid off who should have seen it coming. These people blindly carry on to the last day as if the status quo were stability. Sometimes they subconsciously realize their impending predicament, yet still do something self-destructive, such as buy a new car or house, or they pick a fight with new management precisely when top management is deciding who stays and who goes. Guess what? They end up going.

How can you tell that your tenure may be coming to an end? Some signs to watch for include:

+ You haven't had a promotion in about three years.
+ You're paid more than newer, younger employees doing the same work.
+ Your company is losing market share to its competitors.
+ You've been passed over for an expected promotion, bonus, or raise.
+ Critical job functions previously assigned to you have been reassigned to others.
+ You're not invited to meetings involving your area of responsibility.
+ You have a gut feeling that others are avoiding you.
+ Your boss falls out of favor with top management.
+ Your boss of many years retires, leaving your department leaderless.
+ You get a new boss who is significantly younger than you.
+ Your peers at other companies are being laid off.
+ You're offered an unwanted transfer.
+ Your request to participate in training is ignored.
+ Formerly good performance reviews are suddenly mixed or bad and overly critical.
+ Your request for new business cards (a $25 value) is stalled by your boss.

If several of these signs apply to you, you'd better start planning. Do you see any cause for concern? If so, your first task is to decide whether to fight for your job or prepare to leave.

Here are four steps to take if you really want to stay with your current employer:

1. **Try to get a mission-critical assignment.** Sign on for projects that are central to the survival and success of the company. Become a person who makes things happen instead of a person who just gets by. Diversify into related fields like industrial hygiene, risk management, ergonomics.

   Also consider volunteering for a special-project team. There are a lot of good projects, even in a downsizing environment. Almost all companies that cut back are hiring people at the same time in other areas. Find out where your company needs help and position yourself to provide it.

2. **Communicate your successes.** Make a list of all you've accomplished in the past six months or so, and find ways to disseminate that information to influential people in the organization. A performance review (often a semi-secret document) can serve as an effective tool for doing this. Use your performance reviews to illustrate your creativity and ingenuity to people in the organization who have the authority to boost your reputation. You want to spread the word about what you've contributed and accomplished. This is a beneficial tactic whether you feel threatened or not.

   If your immediate boss is gunning for you, try to inoculate yourself by sharing information around and over him or her. Tread carefully and try not to contradict your boss overtly or do anything that could be construed as backbiting or insubordination. Just kindly, gently, get the word out. Remember that whenever you give credit to your team, you credit yourself as well. There's no need to commandeer all of the glory—that will only nullify the original intent of your memos.

3. **Shore up your skill-set.** Take a hard, honest look at yourself. Are you on top of current industry trends? Is there new technology you've been avoiding? Did you skip some training that others in your field consider standard, like becoming a Certified Safety Professional (CSP)? Have you read the latest business book that your boss and peers are discussing? Do you keep abreast of current business events in the *Wall Street Journal*?

   You may be correct in saying that some trends will disappear without leaving a trace. But now isn't the time for arrogance. If you feel threatened, look for short-term solutions to any skill-set deficiencies. Take a weekend workshop, acquire another credential, or seek coaching from a colleague. But don't sign up for a two-year credentialing program. Look for free vendor demonstrations, not an expensive training program in another city. Make a list of competencies and an action plan to bring your skills up to date. Once again, this strategy serves you whether you stay or leave. You can't compete in today's job market with stale skills.

   You should consider developing one new skill each year. Preferably, it should be a double-duty skill—a skill that both augments your capacity in your current role and could be profitable as a line of work in itself. We all need multiple skills. Then, if one opportunity evaporates, you'll have more than one other skill you can turn to. This could include a part-time job consulting, acting as an expert witness, or teaching.

4. **Get lean and mean.** If you've gotten soft and lazy, come in late, leave early, skip meetings, drink at lunch, or avoid necessary travel, you'll have to change this behavior to keep your job. That might mean putting in more than eight hours a day; it certainly means demonstrating your value and proving your abilities.

The End Can Be a Bitter Pill

If you've decided to leave, or have a pretty strong hunch your position will be eliminated, don't hang on till the bitter end. History demonstrates that the first people out the door are frequently the most self-confident, competent, and highly paid, while everybody who's left is going to have to work three or four times as hard as they did before. Typically, the smart people get out before they're fired, since it's always better to look for work while you have a job. It's also smart not to hit the job market after employers have already seen lots of candidates from your company.

Pending layoffs aren't the only reason for leaving a job. You should leave any time your personal mission and vision aren't in alignment with the company. If you do not agree with the company's mission and vision, you don't belong there. It's a question of fit, timing, and culture.

Two steps to follow once you've decided to leave include:

1. **Dust off your network.** Before doing anything else, revive your network. Most safety professionals don't realize how many people they know. Just go to a professional society meeting or an annual conference and you will see how many professionals you do know—and they know thousands of other people. Create a list of your contacts, including everyone you can think of, ranging from petroleum engineers and insurance professionals to company presidents. Of course, be sure to list every former boss; subordinates and co-workers at your former employers; and every contractor, supplier, customer, and competitor of those employers. These are your best bets for job leads later on, since they know you and your industry.

   Develop your list at the first hint of trouble, not *after* you need a job. We've all gotten an insincere call from some poorly remembered former colleague, begging for help on a job search.

These folks give networking a bad name. So before you call for help, make a friendly contact at least two months earlier if possible. Remember, as a rule, in good economic times it takes about a week per $10,000 in salary to find an equal-paying job (i.e., 8 *weeks* for an $80,000 job), but it takes about a month per $10,000 in salary to find an equal-paying job (i.e., 8 *months* for an $80,000 job) when times are tough.

2. **Have your resume ready**. Everyone you meet will ask for a copy of your resume, and it's only polite to have one handy. It's your calling card, and a good one is worth its weight in gold. So keep some copies of your most recently updated resume in a plain manila envelope and carry them everywhere you go. Living in a state of perpetual readiness may seem tiring, but by being prepared to succeed in the job market, you'll never be permanently hurt if the ax should fall.

Even when your career is going well and you are satisfied, be prepared: Always keep your eyes open for the winds of change—for both the worst and the best.

And, in good times or bad, whether you stay in your present job or find a new one, the steps outlined here will also add polish to any upcoming performance review.

Performance Checkup: How to Make the Most of your Performance Review

When it comes to careers and money, changing jobs isn't the only way to get ahead. It may be time to stop job-jumping and start concentrating on how to make yourself more valuable once you're firmly inside an organization. One way to do that is through the annual performance review, which can be your path to more job security, bigger bonuses, and upward mobility.

What's in It for You?

Performance reviews follow fairly predictable formulas. Every six or 12 months, you meet with your boss and review your achievements based on the written goals and objectives that were established at your last appraisal. If you've done well, you get a raise. If not, you may get a token increase or nothing at all. Some estimate that average raises range from 3 percent to 6 percent—and we're not just talking cash. Compensation can come in the form of stock, telecommuting options, more vacation time, use of the company vacation condo, or a promotion.

Working the Review Process

Since good performance reviews provide an avenue for proving your ongoing value to an organization, don't begin the process the night before you meet with your boss. Start from the day you're hired by establishing goals and performance objectives with your boss. Nail down how each achievement will be quantified and how you'll be rewarded.

Explain your seemingly intangible contribution in dollar terms. Tell your boss how you decreased incident rates, reduced costs, or increased productivity and efficiency. When you go into the review, bring along past reviews (or notes) for reference, evidence of professional education you've received, and compliments you've received from customers and vendors.

Inner Secrets

These tips just scratch the surface. What if your company's stock just dropped 30 percent, but you feel that you still deserve that 10 percent raise or promotion?

Not all merit increases are created equal. Managers are usually given a discretionary budget to apply to their entire group. If you're new or at the lower end of the ladder, you may get a fatter percentage increase than someone closer to the ceiling.

What if your department lacks a fast track for someone as ambitious as you are? Look for ways to boost your qualifications or climb elsewhere in the company. If your organization posts job openings and encourages you to take additional training, do it. This will establish you as someone who is serious about moving up. And when that performance review rolls around, you'll be in a position to signal that you're ready for your next career move, with your boss' help and mentorship. In short, keep one eye on the now (your raise) and another on the future (your career).

What-ifs

Let's assume your review comes at the beginning of the year when financial crises in Asia have yet to be resolved. With many multinational companies facing slumping stock prices, sales, and profitability, will your opportunity at performance-review time shrink?

Not necessarily. Current problems won't necessarily affect basic compensation packages. Companies know that many of their employees have numerous job possibilities. If their compensation packages do not remain competitive, valuable employees may walk across the street.

But with lower profitability and increasing pressure on high wages, companies will definitely look for cutbacks wherever they can. Cost-cutting measures might involve less spending on research and development, cutting some projects altogether, outsourcing some production, and in general becoming more budget-conscious so salaries for high-tech employees remain intact and the company doesn't lose its people.

But what do you do if your scheduled review comes just when your company's stock is getting clobbered and raises are frozen?

Go ahead—even if it's a mock review. You want to go on record as having certain achievements under your belt so when your real review happens when a raise is possible, you'll start from there.

Wrap-up

Your review is done. Maybe you're happy with the results. Then again, maybe you're not. Should you leave after a short stint and increase your paycheck 15 to 20 percent by going elsewhere? Only if your immediate goal is cash. While a job-hopping strategy may work once or twice in hot job markets, constant moves may damage your career, especially if the job demand in your field suddenly turns cold. Try to stay with a firm four to five years so you can rack up some accomplishments. Prove your worth by staying put. It will pay off for the company—and for your career—in the long run.

Now that you have achieved the performance review that suits your performance, you will need to determine how you fit in with the company management and staff. You will need to identify your likability quotient.

Improving Your Likability Quotient

The most likable leader is not necessarily the most sociable, but is someone who treats people with fairness and respect. Some of the most technically proficient, and managerially inept, professionals pride themselves on always getting the job done. They work exhausting hours, never accept defeat, and let no one stand in the way of achieving a goal.

Their motto is "Work hard, play hard." The problem is that their employees never have time to play. These managers don't tolerate the inevitable schedule slippage or equipment failure, so staff members go out of their way to hide problems from them. And since it takes longer to make decisions democratically, these individuals manage from the top down and rarely accept advice. Predictably, they alienate clients, staff, vendors, and consultants—everyone they depend on to achieve their goals.

Not surprisingly, their resumes are now five pages long—a series of 24-month "successes" that are also "failures" because they can't build consensus, loyalty, or ownership. In a nutshell, they have a low LQ, or likability quotient.

What Is Likability?

Likability isn't necessarily about being a nice person. It's about treating people fairly, with respect, promoting teamwork, acknowledging contributions, and rewarding measured risk-taking. It requires personal qualities and a management style that make staff and clients enjoy working with you.

Likability is compatible with, not contradictory to, toughness and determination. People abhor working on a losing team and love to work on a winning team. They don't mind working toward ambitious goals that require personal sacrifice, and most will willingly follow a person they trust and respect.

It follows, therefore, that building likability into your management style can pay real dividends in low turnover, loyalty, high productivity, and morale.

Unfortunately, many executives lower their likability quotient as they move up the ranks to tougher assignments. They believe that if anything is going to get done, they will have to do it, rather than delegating to other qualified professionals. They find it unnecessary to build consensus or create a nurturing environment. Often, they falsely believe that delegating authority or admitting they don't have all the answers will be seen as signs of weakness.

However, the best professionals—those who command most of the top jobs in the successful organizations—are able to achieve ambitious objectives without creating misery and disruption in the ranks. They remain likable.

So, how can you increase your likability quotient?

- Keep in mind that good employees want to do a good job, but need to know what that job is. I have discovered that 50 percent of all communications are misunderstood. So communicate your expectations often and clearly.
- Accept that two heads can produce more ideas and solutions than one. *Your job is not to do all the thinking, but to make others think.* Your job is to manage and bring closure to the thought process.
- Provide honest performance feedback. Give praise when warranted (in public when possible) and constructive criticism when appropriate (in private), but keep criticism impersonal and related to the job.
- Make everyone a stakeholder in a project's success or failure. Communication about progress and a clear definition of responsibilities establish a mutual sense of ownership.
- Spread the recognition around. Leadership is taking a little more of the blame, a little less of the credit, and doing a lot more of the work. So, don't take all the credit. Let others bask in the glory of their accomplishments and know that their hard work will also be recognized.
- Try to absorb much of the pressure. People are intimidated by high-level tantrums, and providing some political shelter keeps them positively focused and reassured.
- Be visible. There is a direct correlation between your likability and accessibility. You'll also stay better informed. This is also known as management by walking around (MBWA), a term coined by Tom Peters.

+ Provide leadership. Set and communicate goals, monitor results, give pep talks, and set high standards. People want and need to follow a leader, but it must be one they can respect. So you need to be the example of integrity.

There is no single model for achieving likability. A style that is effective in an engineering firm probably won't fly in a manufacturing company. However, building respect and trust works everywhere, and elements of effective management and leadership are fairly universal. So follow the golden rule and manage others as you want to be managed.

What's Your Excuse for Procrastinating?

It has been said that there are two callers in life we absolutely *must* answer to on schedule: Neither the taxman nor the Grim Reaper will be put off. Everyone and everything else we can put off—and usually do. Procrastination is an almost universal peccadillo. And like a head cold that is hardly disastrous (but annoying, nonetheless), we can live with procrastination, but we'd really love to be rid of it.

Procrastination is actually rationalization in action (or *inaction*). Procrastination is not thrust on us. We will it into being. It will probably never go away entirely, but if we can catalog our favorite excuses, then we can take a solid first step toward combating the off-putting habit of putting things off.

As a sometimes procrastinator myself, I've used most available excuses, and I find that they can usually be placed into four categories.

1. **Distractions.** We procrastinate on tasks we dislike. We seldom, if ever, put off things that are fun. These are dis-

tractions, and while they feel pretty good when we give in to them, we usually end up flaying ourselves later when the fun ends and our job still needs to be done. It's difficult to say *no* to the lure of a pleasant distraction. However, reminding ourselves that we'll feel a bit better with the job out of the way (while also freeing ourselves up to have fun later) can often be enough to carry us through. Pleasant distractions include getting asked to help with the United Way campaign, planning a week of activities during the drive. We'll do this *instead of* updating our Hazard Communication Program or our Spill Plan, or writing another piece of the Risk Management Plan for next year. Yuck! Details, details, details. But they all need to be done.

2. **Something else—better, more important—came up.** This is the first cousin to distractions, but requires more than your average dose of rationalization. To honestly succeed in putting the job off with this one, the intruding activity has to actually be more important than the job at hand. Something better could be an optional meeting you attend on wellness instead of doing your monthly statistics. Something more important could be conducting an audit of a facility your company is buying rather than calculating the incident rate for last year (which is due at the end of the month) based on some weird algorithm a particular trade organization uses rather than your company standard. Beat this efficiency killer by promising yourself at the outset of your task, that nothing is more important than finishing the job. Then simply keep your promise. Your word is good, right?

3. **It's somebody else's fault.** So this wasn't supposed to be your job in the first place. So somebody blew it somewhere

along the line and this rotten job landed right smack dab in your lap. And now you're steamed. You've got four choices: (1) complain, (2) refuse to do the job, (3) complain, or (4) do it. The first three choices take more time and energy than the fourth. Also, they leave you smoldering in somebody else's bad graces. On the other hand, performing the task quickly, quietly, humbly, and well, earns you kudos and lots of respect.

4. **Couldn't get motivated.** Safety professionals love this one. "When I have spare time, I don't want to waste it on _____ (insert your boring task). In the real world this simply means that no one has cracked the whip, or explained the consequences of procrastinating. The boredom disappears when someone dumps a drop-dead deadline on you— like tomorrow. It may be tough to drag yourself to the dentist for a cleaning, but it sure beats dragging yourself to the dentist later for a root canal. Reviewing and submitting your Spill Prevention Control Countermeasures to the Department of Environmental Quality (DEQ) is difficult because you have to organize and schedule a meeting with three different groups, collect the comments, revise the plan and circulate it for signatures, then submit it to the DEQ. Sometimes I think I would rather go to the dentist.

Self-motivation is hard, yes, but it's easier if you picture the welter of trouble you might be bringing on yourself later if you don't crank up your willpower and get to work now.

By the way, if you decided to read this chapter at first glance, rather than leaving it for later, congratulations!

Quickly now, move on to the next task, before something better distracts you.

Managing Change and Going With The Flow

When her company hastily called a meeting to announce deep budget cuts and even deeper layoffs, a company executive said that she felt as if "suddenly, there was no gravity—it was sucked right out of the room." That's how chilling a close encounter with sudden, uninvited change feels. And yet big changes loom everywhere: from the size of your company (or team) to your core business, from the corporate pecking order to the very definition of employment. Even companies that are doing well are not immune to the fidgets and jitters change produces.

That means the managers who do the tough work of leading people through change can't simply hand out copies of the latest marketing plan or pick up a few pointers at a seminar. More is required. But where should they begin? As veterans of change will tell you, the better you understand the topography of the change process, the more sure-footed you'll be when you find yourself in the middle of it. Here are four ways to tackle change:

1. **Don't be afraid to talk about failure.** It may sound strange to say that success depends on failure, but it does. Failure is a touchy subject for individuals as well as for companies, the armed forces, and even for countries. But every failed enterprise or project is a lesson: Only through countless trial and lots of error do we move ahead and come up with something new.

2. **Practice failure.** A Silicon Valley computer company president once startled the employees by proclaiming "If you're not making ten mistakes a day, you're not trying hard enough!" A little macho, maybe, but exactly the kind of bossy behavior I adore. If you can't imagine aiming for ten mistakes a day, you can practice failure a little at a time.

To take the sting out of defeat, begin with small stakes and small losses. Try a couple of personal things where success, though not guaranteed, is not far away: Swim two extra laps tomorrow, attempt a complicated recipe, try out some new software. Next, try something at work: Propose a product enhancement or a way to improve customer service, suggest that you head up a high-profile project. You will discover, to your surprise, that disappointment, if it comes, might not feel great, but it won't kill you.

3. **Do what you are afraid to do.** If you can muster the nerve to see what's gaining on you, a measure of courage results; you'll see that a hardy spirit (yours) can be coaxed forth. For instance, face what polls say is Americans' number-one fear: Enroll in a public speaking course—then sit down and watch yourself making a speech on videotape. Or get serious about an avocation: Enroll in an Outward Bound program for a weekend. Wear red.

4. **Manage brain power.** The fancy name for this is "knowledge management," but let's just say that, unless you know what talent lurks in your workforce and how to tap into it, you're sunk. Putting knowledge-management strategies to work involves assessing *intellectual assets*, including creativity, communication ability, and analytical and problem-solving skills. Widespread conversations help in this assessment, but you should think about this systematically.

   To take the first step in this direction, sit down privately with each person who reports to you. (Save performance appraisals for another day; they look back in time, and the idea is to look ahead.) Find out what each employee can do, what abilities are lying fallow, what skills each individual wants to acquire over, say, the next year, and how that acquisition would contribute to your company. When you're done, you'll have a much clearer picture of the potential that resides in your team.

Change happens fast. Then people everywhere are scrambling to adjust, and that takes time. The worst sin managers can commit is to blame *their* troubles on foot-dragging, change-averse employees. So stop complaining about negative employee attitudes. Ask yourself: Would I want this change applied to my job? If your answer is yes, start with yourself first. Make some visible changes. You will set a splendid example.

"Dem Bones"

Certainly, at some point in your life you've heard the song, "Dem Bones." But did you know that some people actually exhibit characteristics of certain bones as they manage their careers and the personnel who work for them? Think about it.

As you can probably surmise, there are several ways to use this bone metaphor that can help you manage your own career:

+ Wish Bones
+ Back Bones
+ Funny Bones

Wish Bones

As a safety manager you should be dreaming about things to ask for, or programs to implement in the future. This is essentially a *wish list*. It should convey a vision of the future that helps establish organizational cohesion and acts as a catalyst to define the organization's mission and potential. This wish list can provide the seminal impetus for a long-range and strategic plan for your department. The plan can be used to guide you and your department, while ensuring a modicum of security. So when someone asks what you are doing and where your department is going, your employees can confidently communicate such a direction.

Every safety manager should have a vision. Without a vision you might perish. With a vision—and your wish bones—your department can flourish.

Wish bones can also take on a more contentious aspect. Employees proclaim, "I wish we could do this. . . . " or "Why don't we do that? . . ." Generally speaking, they are more adept at asking the questions and throwing rocks at other people's programs, but are far less adept at recommending improvements. Even when they offer a suggestion, they are not willing to assist in implementing it.

Back Bones

Any good manager must have a strong spine. Many managers are more like snails and rubber chickens because they lack a spine. These people have frustrated me terribly. They stand up for nothing and are quick to go with the flow. Being a safety manager with a strong spine is sometimes an occupational hazard (no pun intended). When you stand up for what is right, you sometimes sit down at another job. Do you have the guts to have a backbone to stand up for what is right and true?

Funny Bones

Almost everyone likes to laugh occasionally. Employees and bosses alike enjoy a chuckle once in a while. People generally want to be part of a positive, fun activity. Be the positive person that people like to see coming because you are a joy to be around, whether you are bearing good news or bad.

It is also true that *negatively* "funny" people tend to suck the energy out of you and give you a frontal lobe headache. People with these funny bones typically wear their feelings on their sleeves. They tell you everything that they don't like in the form of a joke. That way when you challenge them or call them on the carpet, you get the well-prepared response, "Hey, I was only joking! Why are you taking it so seriously?" The only thing that amuses you as the manager is when they leave the company.

Other Bones

Every organization also has people who exhibit traits of other bones:

+ Jaw Bones
+ Dry Bones

Jaw Bones

Jaw bones refer to those who talk a lot—whether productive or counterproductive. They are always concerned with this deal or that deal, or what is happening over in that department, rather than focusing on their own job. They tend to be contentious gossipers. Contrary to popular stereotypes, they can be men as easily as women. They stir up strife, emotions, and turmoil, making the manager's job much more difficult.

Dry Bones

Dry bones refer to people who look very good on the outside but are very stale on the inside. They may be the "twenty-year" people who have put in the same year twenty times, just getting by. Or, it could be that they are burned out, have personal problems, or have no spark for a variety of other reasons. Regardless, they look good on the outside but are dead on the inside. You will need to revitalize these dry bones—bring them back to life—or help them find another job, possibly with another company.

Making the Break from Middle Manager to Executive Manager

What does it take to slip through that narrow, upwardly bound, but quickly closing elevator door from middle manager to the Grand Pooh-Bah ranks of the senior executive manager? This is a question many have tried to answer. It is an issue many have debated. It has polarized the masses, those who consider leaders versus managers, nature versus nurture, performance versus politics, style over substance, and who you know versus what you know.

Some of the characteristics that separate the wheat from the chaff are:

+ **Strategic thinking.** This means that you have a business sense for seamlessly integrating safety, health, and environmental (SHE) issues into the business process. Every strategic opportunity is viewed as an opportunity to move the discipline forward.
+ **Persuasiveness.** Being able to persuade upper management as well as employees is essential to your success in moving to upper management. If you are viewed as one of them and think like they do, they will want you to be around, because you understand them.
+ **Political adroitness.** Knowing when to speak and when not to speak, what to do and what not to do, where to be and where not to be are key in moving to upper management. Success is all in the timing: being in the right place, at the right time, and having the right words to say.
+ **Broad awareness.** It is clear that moving up the ladder of management requires a *forest* viewpoint rather than a *tree* viewpoint of business. Having the macrovision is viewed more favorably than the myopic microvision.

+ **A sense of humor.** Fast-trackers effectively use this approach to soften tough messages and relieve stress.
+ **Time-management skills.** If time manages you, you will never get things done. It has been said that time is like a gift, that is why they call it the present.
+ **The ability to set priorities.** To be able to sort through the noise and stay on target is extraordinarily useful.
+ **Ethics.** This is obvious. If your gut-check tells you *no*, don't do it.
+ **Teamwork.** We all know that team players are viewed more favorably than rock throwers. Being a team player can get you to upper management and keep you there.
+ **Industry knowledge.** Having a command of the industry is critical if you are to deal with people who work in the field on a daily basis.
+ **Interpersonal skills.** Without the proper interpersonal skills you may not last long at middle management, much less achieve upper management
+ **Problem-solving ability.** Being able to solve the company's big problems efficiently and with business savvy will definitely open the doors to upper management.
+ **The drive to excel.** Earn respect for being exceptionally good at what you do. This comes from experience and a proven track record at this and other companies.
+ **Respect.** Another obvious, positive trait. Treat people the way you would like to be treated, even if your peers do not. More people will want to work with you, and it builds others' respect for you.
+ **Initiative.** Show that you can manage your discipline independently. Deliver results without a lot of hand-holding.
+ **Superior communications skills.** Can you write proposals, stand in front of a group and give presentations? Some have lost the opportunity because they failed here.

+ **Consistency in behavior.** Don't fly off the handle. Others expect predictability in how you respond in different situations, whether minor or major.
+ **Consistency in decision making.** This assumes that you make decisions in the first place. Upper management is always looking for people to take charge and make decisions, to be consistent in making good decisions, and to make decisions predictably based on the requisite conditions.
+ **Willingness to tackle the biggest tasks.** Be able to assess risk and have a plan B ready. Volunteer for important projects or task forces. You will be noticed by other members of the management team and get cross-functional knowledge that you might not get within your own department.
+ **Self-confidence.** Talk to your boss as a peer. Developing a relationship is a huge issue. Does your boss feel comfortable around you?
+ **Flexibility.** Take operating and administrative jobs to broaden your knowledge and strive to see things from other points of view.
+ **Concentration.** Continually seek feedback. A lot of people read a lot of books and go to a lot of classes. If you've got a lot of head knowledge, why aren't you moving up? It is usually because you are using a shotgun rather than a .22 caliber to get the focused training.
+ **Chemistry.** After all the talk about knowledge and capabilities, the advancement decision boils down to a chemistry between you and the executive manager. This sometimes means proving you belong in the club. It sometimes means you can get results and not embarrass the senior executive who hired you. And sometimes it even hinges on whether you are entertaining and fun to hang out with.

As you move up the corporate ladder, you will need to add a new skill set to your portfolio, that is, understanding safety as a business function. Safety is no longer that altruistic discipline of preventing people from getting injured on the job. If you are to succeed here you must understand the way corporate leaders think and implement safety in terms they understand. There are no college courses that teach these principles.

Safety as a Business Function

After the Cherry Picking, What Next?

You've just celebrated one year without a lost-time injury. Everyone is patting you on the back for a job well done. You've successfully changed much of the culture from negative to positive. You are enjoying your day in the sun, a sign that you got everyone from employees to top management to buy into and make the safety program work. As you are about to bask in the glory and shift into cruise control, your plant manager approaches. He says, "Good job for the last two years. I'm really pleased with your hard work. But how do you top what you just did? Think about where you want to be next year, okay? By the way, let's sit down next Monday and talk about it." You reply, "Sir, I've given that a lot of thought, and I'd love to sit down and talk to you about it!" But inside you are screaming, "Ah-Ah-Ah-Ah-Ah! Someone Help Me!" You just went from elated to terrified. What's a safety manager to do?

Well, if you were a planner, you would have presented your pre-approved plan at the celebration. It's too late for that now. You must examine where you are and where you want to go. You've done all the easy things. You've written a comprehensive safety program, completed the first comprehensive audit, changed the culture. Everything on the surface looks squared away. Now the job gets harder. Your boss expects you to be a visionary and to formulate a plan for the next quantum leap. But what is a visionary?

When you examine where you are and where you want to go, you must make some well-thought-out decisions and present a cogent plan that looks like, well, you have your stuff together. Do this wrong and you might be considered a flash in the pan, pigeon-holed in this job with no hope for ever moving up, or worse yet, put on a makeshift raft headed towards the front gate. Yikes! After all the recent success! How could they do that?! It happens all the time. So be cautious and think carefully about what you want to do. It could cost you your job; at a minimum, it could cost you your future advancement.

What Is a Visionary?

One of *Webster's* definitions of a visionary is "disposed to reverie or imagining, illusory; dreamy." My definition of a visionary is someone who understands the past and present and has an idea of what the future will hold. *Webster's* offers two key words: imagining and dreamy. The first implies using imagination, innovation, and creativity. It means more than merely hanging on from year to year. Dreamy means making your wish list. Martin Luther King did not galvanize civil rights advocates with, "I have an objective"; he did it with the phrase, "I have a dream."

I can't tell you how many times I have run into safety professionals and asked them what their five-year plan is. The reply is generally, "Gee, I haven't given that much thought. I'm just trying to get through this year." However, when I ask, "What would you do if you won the lottery?" the reply is "I'm going to buy a new house, a new car, a winter (or summer) home, retire and write books," and on and on. If safety professionals would only apply the same energy to their professional aspirations as they do to their personal dreams, who knows what they could achieve?

Choices to Make

Let's take a look at some of the options you could choose from (or even mix and match). What items you choose from this shopping list to make the next quantum leap depend largely on your particular company. You could integrate safety with the International Organization for Standardization's (ISO) 9000 quality management systems standard, pursue OSHA's Voluntary Protection Program (VPP) status, increase audits, increase visibility of the safety department, increase training, or incorporate environmental issues.

1. **Integrate safety with ISO 9000.** ISO 9000 is replete with safety, health, and environmental references. If your company is pursuing these various certifications, embed your safety goals and objectives in these quality measures. For example:

   Quality: the totality of features and characteristics of a product or service that bear on its ability to satisfy stated or implied needs. . . . Needs are usually translated into features and characteristics with specific criteria (which) may include aspects of usability, **safety**, availability, maintainability, economics, and **environment** (ISO 8402-1986, Section 3.1, draft ISO/DIS 8402, Section 2.1, and ANSI/ASQC A3-1987, Section 2.1).

From the very outset, embed your safety goals and objectives into all of the ISO 9000 criteria. This will further cement the focus on safety in the facility.

2. **Pursue VPP Status.** If you are not a VPP site, examine which one is more applicable, Merit, Star, or Demonstration. Look at the nineteen elements and forge a plan to put programs in place. If you decide to pursue this status, you may need corporate support. Get the corporate staff behind you and then approach management.

3. **Increase audits.** This may sound nit-picking; however, when you take your audits below the surface, you find out if things really happen like they are supposed to happen. You may find that, when you scratch away the surface-level paint, everything is held together with bubble gum and baling wire, and that it's very tenuous. Also, taking a *closer* look at audits forces you to attend to the details. We often miss the details because we are in such a hurry to finish the audit and get the report out. You may unearth some interesting truths that did not come out in the original audit.

Changing your assessment activities from the required schedule to a more aggressive schedule may assist in improving your safety program. For example, if an item is required to be inspected annually, do it semi-annually. Audit the inspection forms to assure that they are completed accurately. Look at the corrective actions and see if all of the changes have been completed on a monthly basis.

If your site is covered by Process Safety Management (PSM), and you really want to be thorough, audit the mechanical integrity program. That should entail enough work to keep you busy for several years. By the way, do you also have an electrical integrity program? Mechanical integrity is the heart of a PSM program in that it fixes problems before they occur and, in many cases, averts catastrophic events. Audit the high-frequency incidents to make sure that the workplace has been engineered to prevent recurrence and that procedures have been changed to reflect the additional precautions.

Audit the hazardous operations to ensure that all the bases are covered, from employee participation to pre-start-up safety reviews. Examine the changes to process and instrument drawings to ensure that design changes were penned. Then go out in the field and verify that the changes were actually made. Sound like a lot of work? You bet it is, but it will definitely ensure that quantum leap you want.

4. **Increase visibility of the safety department.** What does this mean? Well, it means YOU need to get out of your office and walk around the facility—not weekly, but daily. Every day you and your staff need to be seen by as many people as possible. Since employees don't eat, drink, and sleep safety like you do, seeing you reminds them to work safely. This may require additional staff to cover two or three shifts.

5. **Increase training.** One way to improve safety is to increase the training for line supervision. For example, the National Safety Council provides a course called "The Safety-Trained Supervisor." When supervisors are aware of all the reasons behind what you do, it will help immensely. Also, they will have a greater appreciation for what safety managers do and why they do it.

6. **Incorporate environmental issues.** Every day more titles link environmental and safety concerns together rather than apart. Safety and environmental issues have a natural relationship, even though there are some differences. Cooperate closely with the environmental department and work the synergies.

Now you have a taste of what a plan could consist of; apply it to your career by developing a plan of your own. Then, once you are done with the cherry picking, look for those areas where you can get the most mileage out of small improvements. Keep refining your objectives so that you can realize your goal as a safety professional—preventing people from incurring injury and illness.

Value-added Safety: Adding Value Without Using the Word "Compliance"

If the word "compliance" were removed from the dictionary, how many safety professionals would continue to effectively implement safety for their companies? In fact, how many safety professionals would still have a job without the cloud of governmental compliance for safety looming over their company's heads—especially those who claim they were hired "in case OSHA shows up"? It is unfortunate that many safety professionals seem to gravitate to *negative* rather than *positive* methods to get management's attention.

Let's go one step further: What if the word "compliance" were replaced by the term "value added"? The cloud might darken because safety at your company is a cost center rather than a profit center. Instead of implementing OSHA-mandated procedures, you would have to demonstrate how following these procedures adds value.

Finally, what if OSHA were abolished altogether? In light of OSHA reform, surely many safety professionals have wondered what would happen if OSHA were off the radar screen. Without OSHA, would you not have to show up for work tomorrow because there are no government regulations? Or would you still be around because you make things better by adding value?

What Is Value-added Safety?

Let's define this animal. First, "value added" refers to taking an item, such as a piece of equipment, a product, a process, or something similar, and making it better; thus, increasing its value. From a safety standpoint, it refers to making that item inherently safer, more useful, and easier to use, without sacrificing quality. Does an end-product have less potential for injury? Does a process use less hazardous materials? Are there fewer steps in a chemical process, thereby reducing potential employee exposure? These are things that add value and increase quality from a safety standpoint.

Value-added safety also refers to doing something better and faster while maintaining safety and increasing productivity. For example, a company brings in three large trucks of hazardous chemicals for a process. The chemical is unloaded and metered into the process following the recipe. This takes 8-10 hours per truck and requires employees to continuously monitor the transfer, as well as wear all the required personal protective equipment (PPE) (not much fun, especially in August in the Gulf Coast area). Let's say these same three trucks can be loaded into a storage tank at a peak rate of about 4 hours for all three trucks combined. The chemical is then later metered into the process via a closed system. This frees up employees to do other things, takes less time for truck drivers to unload the chemical, and reduces exposure to the chemical. As a result, value is added to the process by making tasks easier to perform and providing less exposure for the company. Nowhere did you find the word *compliance* in this scenario, even though the chemical exposure was reduced significantly.

Looking at another situation, let's say you want to implement a deluge system that costs $8,000. If a catastrophic failure were to occur, we could look at business interruption costs; loss of product;

loss of product quality; potential environmental ramifications if the reportable quantity were reached; and exposure to personnel, neighboring facilities, and residences. What about the cost of equipment damage or emergency response from the company, other neighboring companies, and local fire departments? When considering these costs, adding a deluge system clearly adds value to the company operations.

Do your procedures add value? Are tasks easier to perform rather than harder? Granting that OSHA-mandated procedures require many specific steps and PPE, how do we as professionals make these tasks as easy as possible? *Do your programs add value?* Are they guidelines to make tasks easier or rules to restrict employees from doing things wrong? *Do you add value?* Or do you warm a seat waiting for OSHA to show up and justify your existence? If you are waiting for OSHA to show up, it may be a long time before they do, if ever. If OSHA were abolished tomorrow, would you get a call to stay home because you were retired early or—worse yet—fired because there was no regulatory reason for your existence? In this day of re-engineering, you know that this could happen. You need to think about how you can add value rather than detract from it without using the word *compliance.*

Dollars and Sense of Safety Programs: Using Financial Principles in the Safety Profession

If safety were confined only to ensuring that the appropriate systems and programs were present, all of our jobs would be exceedingly enjoyable. However, safety involves not only engineering design and management, but also financial planning, budgeting, marketing, and business. We are not only required to write, implement, and maintain safety and health programs, but also to manage people, activities, and tasks so that they get done in an orderly fashion—that is, on schedule and within budgetary constraints.

We are placed in a position that requires us to market and manage even *before* we are given the go-ahead to implement safety programs. We all know the reasons why a good company needs safety and health management systems. But we are often faced with the dilemma of convincing unschooled superiors to accept the monetary costs of these systems.

Understanding this requires that we change our plan of attack. We were *not* hired because our companies were altruistic about providing an environment where employees did not get hurt. We were *not* hired because our companies were enamored with safety. However, we *were* hired because it makes good business sense. We *were* hired to reduce the costs of workers' compensation, the medical costs resulting from injuries, and the costs of potential OSHA citations. So it's easy to see why safety has been labeled a cost center.

Employers are in business to do one thing, make money. If they don't make money, they won't stay in business. Once safety professionals come to grips with this reality, it makes the road to successful health and safety planning much smoother. The following are ways I've discovered to sell safety and health based on sound financial principles, that is, from a monetary viewpoint as well as from an altruistic viewpoint.

1. **Identify Costs**. Find out where money is being spent. Is it being wasted? Is it accomplishing your goals? Are you getting the best value for your dollar?

   Before you can determine what safety items should be purchased, the current safety equipment and budget should be analyzed. Include in this review the current costs for safety equipment in use (safety glasses, prescription safety glasses, goggles, boots, gloves, acid suits, flame-resistant clothing, hard hats, hearing protection, emergency medical equipment, etc.) as well as the cost for capital equipment (sprinkler systems, firefighting equipment, training courses, upgrades identified from insurance audits, etc.). Once you have identified where all of your safety expenditures are going, try to determine a more efficient way to spend your budget dollar. For example, some employers use contractors to maintain first-aid cabinets at a monthly cost. By mail ordering the medical supplies and stocking the first-aid cabinets yourself (which will increase your visibility), this cost can be minimized.

2. **Illustrate Control of Costs.** When you treat your department like a business, your desire to control costs will be apparent. Actions like changing vendors or rescheduling calibrations for instruments can accent your fiduciary responsibility. When you have a monetary budget, it is always a good idea to plan on finishing the project on schedule and under budget. It is also a good idea to let upper management know that you were able to return some of the allocated funds. If you don't market yourself, generally speaking, nobody else will. The bottom line is to do as much as possible with your budget dollar without sacrificing the value you are receiving.

Another way to visibly illustrate cost control is to include noncapital expenditure items in your safety budgeting that require little or no financial support, such as working with engineers to help design a safety interlock or a machine guard, or doing field evaluations yourself rather than budgeting for extra manpower. Coupling an extensive safety budget with such clearly beneficial low-cost actions may help your department avoid being labeled as wasteful or indulgent.

3. **Use the Standards to Your Advantage in Budgeting.** Once
    you have identified your costs and shown that you are con-
    trolling them, the next step in safety planning is to tie the
    budgeted items to an applicable standard. There are stan-
    dards established for every industry sector by agencies such
    as OSHA, the Environmental Protection Agency (EPA), Amer-
    ican National Standards Institute (ANSI), National Fire Pro-
    tection Association (NFPA), Underwriters Limited (UL), and
    National Electrical Manufacturing Association (NEMA).
    There are also industry-specific standards. Standards re-
    quired for the petrochemical industry are established by the
    American Petroleum Institute (API), Chemical Manufactur-
    er's Association (CMA), Synthetic Organic Chemical Manu-
    facturers Association (SOCMA), and the American Institute
    of Chemical Engineers (AIChE). The aerospace industry
    uses military (MIL) standards such as, MIL-STD-882,
    MIL-STD-1574, MIL-STD-454, Air Force Regulations (AFRs),
    and Air Force Occupational Safety and Health (AFOSH)
    standards.

These standards spell out almost everything required to make
facilities safe. USE THEM! Then you will be able to show that
everything you are doing is directly linked to compliance. If
upper management elects not to approve a measure, remind them
of the specific compliance reference for that item. Make those
managers with fiduciary power *accountable* for their decisions:
Provide a sign-off list that physically requires top management
to sign or initial for every budgeted safety item (on the prover-
bial bottom line) whether to spend the money or accept the risk
of not spending the money. See the following example for Level
A suits for HAZMAT.

Example

Budget Item #6. HAZMAT Level A Suits for Emergency Response Team: $ 2,360.00 (OSHA 29 CFR 1910.120(H)&(c)(5).

Tychem 10000 Level A Suits (4 @ $500.00) $ 2,000.00
Training Suits (4 @ $90.00) $ 360.00

In the case of a hazardous chemical spill, company policy is to have a minimum of two Emergency Response Team (ERT) members respond, with two standing by as backup. The Level A suits provide the minimum requirements for responding to such an emergency. The use of training suits provide our ERT members with the opportunity to become familiar with the chemical suits prior to an incident and to minimize panic in an emergency situation. Each ERT member should be trained in these suits and in self-contained breathing apparatus (SCBAs).

Implement as Stated Above:
Concur: HR__ Date__ MGR__ Date__ PRES__ Date__

Accept Risk of Criteria 2, Freq 2 = 2:
Concur: HR__ Date__ MGR__ Date__ PRES__ Date__

Also, provide an appendix with the referenced standards. To aid in selling, highlight (as shown below) the particular references to illustrate exactly where the standard supports your proposal.

1910.120 Title: Hazardous Waste Operations and Emergency Response

(a) Scope, application, and definitions . . .

(iii) Voluntary clean-up operations at sites recognized by federal, state, local or other governmental bodies as uncontrolled hazardous waste sites;

(iv) Operations involving hazardous waste that are conducted at treatment, storage, disposal (TSD) facilities regulated by 40 CFR Parts 264 and 265 pursuant to RCRA; or by agencies under agreement with U.S.E.P.A. to implement RCRA regulations; and

(v) Emergency response operations for releases of, or substantial threats of releases of, hazardous substances without regard to the location of the hazard. (2) Application. (i) All requirements of Part 1910 and Part 1926 of Title 29 of the Code of Federal Regulations apply pursuant to their terms to hazardous waste and **emergency response operations whether covered by this section or not. If there is a conflict or overlap, the provision more protective of employee safety and health shall apply without regard to 29 CFR 1910.5(c)(1).**

(ii) Hazardous substance clean-up operations within the scope of paragraphs (a)(1)(i) through (a)(1)(iii) of this section must comply with all paragraphs of this section except paragraphs (p) and (q) ...

(b) Safety and health program.

Note to (b): Safety and health programs developed and implemented to meet other federal, state, or local regulations are considered acceptable in meeting this requirement if they cover or are modified to cover the topics required in this paragraph. An additional or separate safety and health program is not required by this paragraph.

(1) General. (i) Employers shall develop and implement a written safety and health program for their employees involved in hazardous waste operations. The program shall be designed to identify, evaluate, and control safety and health hazards, and provide for emergency response for hazardous waste operations.

(ii) The written safety and health program shall incorporate the following:

(A) An organizational structure;

(B) A comprehensive workplan;

(C) A site-specific safety and health plan which need not repeat the employer's standard operating procedures required in paragraph (b)(1)(ii)(F) of this section;

(D) The safety and health training program.

(5) Personal protective equipment (PPE) shall be provided and used during initial site entry in accordance with the following requirements:

(i) Based upon the results of the preliminary site evaluation, an ensemble of PPE shall be selected and used during initial site entry which will provide protection to a level of exposure below permissible exposure limits and published exposure levels for known or suspected hazardous substances and health hazards and which will provide protection against other known and suspected hazards identified during the preliminary site evaluation. If there is no permissible exposure limit or published exposure level, the employer may use other published studies and information as a guide to appropriate personal protective equipment.

Use Engineering/Financial Principles

Did you ever wonder why the CEO's or comptroller's eyes glassed over when you talked about incident rates and EMRs? For the same reason your eyes glassed over when they talked about return on investments (ROIs) and an equivalent uniform annual cost (EUAC). To communicate with financial planners, you must learn to speak the language that upper management understands—dollars and cents. You must cogently persuade upper management to separate money from their corporate wallets by illustrating why spending money now will save money later. Engineering/economic principles such as present worth, future worth, depreciation, rate of return, replacement, retirement, and cost-benefit analysis are understood by both engineers and financial planners. Use expenditure analyses that illustrate the reduction in your Workers' Compensation experience modifier as a result of incident-rate reduction (or show an increase to recommend not spending the money). Also, the use of insurance audits and reports that reveal the need to upgrade or provide additional equipment can be helpful in justifying expenditures.

Present Worth. The present worth of an asset is the sum of all discounted expected future cash inflows minus the sum of all cash outflows and discounted expected future cash outflows. Restated in simple terms, this means that the value of a machine, or a chemical plant, or an improvement in a process, or other variable is simply the sum total of all the money you expect to make or save over the life of the asset minus present and future costs associated with that asset with everything adjusted for inflation, so that current monetary value is accurately reflected. Present worth is an easy check for the feasibility of a project; projects with negative net present worths can be easily identified and eliminated in favor of those projects with better return potentials. The formula for present worth is:

$$P = \frac{[A(1+i)^n - 1]}{[i(1+i)^n]}$$

where

P = Sum of money at the present time
i = Interest rate for a given interest period

A = A payment or receipts at the end of an interest period in a
       series of n equal payments or receipts
n = number of years.

This is a function of

- ✦ Initial cost or investment
- ✦ Cash outflows such as maintenance costs, time payments,
  and the cost of:
  - Safety program implementation (e.g., confined space,
    lockout/tagout, etc.)
  - Equipment (e.g., fire extinguishers, fire protection, etc.)
  - Training
  - New employees (e.g., safety professionals, industrial
    hygienists, etc.)
- ✦ Cash inflows such as cost savings or payments for goods
  and services and expected:
  - Worker's compensation and insurance savings
  - Decrease in overtime, productivity, turnover, training
    costs, etc.
  - Decrease in legal liabilities, legal fees, settlements
  - Decrease in OSHA citations
  - Increase in good will (e.g., company reputation, union
    negotiating, etc.)
- ✦ Salvage value of the asset
- ✦ Adjustment for inflation (discounting).

Example
In three years, $400,000 will be required for an EPA modification to
your plant. How much money should you invest at 10 percent
to have the required amount when needed? Using the formula

$$P = \frac{[A\,(1 + i)^n - 1]}{[i(1 + i)^n]}$$

where

P = Sum of money at the present time **(the unknown variable)**

i = Interest rate for a given interest period **(10%)**

A = A payment or receipts at the end of an interest period in a series of *n* equal payments or receipts **($400,000)**

n = number of years **(3)**

then

$$P = \frac{[\$400{,}000\,(1 + 0.10)^3 - 1]}{[0.10(1 + 0.10)^3]}$$

P = $300,526.

That is, to have $400,000 in three years with a current interest rate of 10 percent, your company must be able to invest $300,526 now to be able to make the allocated expenditure for EPA modifications at your plant.

Why is it beneficial to be able to illustrate to your management that you can perform this calculation? Well, the allocation calls for a $400,000 expenditure. However, the current investment required is about $100,000 less than the planned target expenditure. This makes good fiduciary sense, especially if you know that these modifications are going to be required. Being able to make these calculations is important; however, knowing *why* and *what* the calculations *mean* is even more important.

Future Worth. The future worth of an asset is the current value of the asset plus the compound interest thereon. This value is also a good check for the feasibility of a project. It can be discounted to present worth in order to compare the value of a product or project with the investment necessary to create it. If the value is less than the investment required, the project should be terminated in favor of more profitable projects. The formula for future worth is:

$$F = P(1 + i)^n$$

where

F = Future worth of a present sum of money after n interest periods, or the future worth of a series of equal payments
P = The sum of money at the present time
i = Interest rate for a given interest period
n = Number of years.

This is a function of

+ Initial value of investment
+ Interest rates (compounding), which are comprised of:
  - True cost of borrowing money (2–3%)
  - Risk of investment/project (junk bonds verses AAA bonds)
  - Rate of inflation (currently somewhere on the order of 3–6% annually, depending on whom you talk to).

Example

Your company may need to install pollution-abatement equipment in three years to bring the facility up to EPA specifications. After speaking with vendors and accountants, you estimate that at that time, $2 million will be needed to make the necessary improvements. Currently, interest rates are at 10 percent and you have $750,000 to set aside and invest in anticipation of spending needs in three years. What will the future worth of $750,000 be and how much will you have to borrow to make up the difference? Using the formula

$F = P(1 + i)^n$

where

F = Future worth of a present sum of money after n interest periods, or the future worth of a series of equal payments **(the unknown variable)**
P = The sum of money at the present time **($750,000)**

i = Interest rate for a given interest period **(10%)**

n = Number of years **(3)**

then

F = $750,000 (1 + 0.10)^3

F = $998,250.

If you will need $2,000,000 for the entire project and you anticipate having $998,250, then you will need to borrow $1,001,750.

How does it benefit you to be able to illustrate to management that you can perform this calculation? Because saving $750,000 in preparation for a $2,000,000 expenditure three years from now shows forethought and vision.

Depreciation. Depreciation is the process of allocating, in a systematic and rational manner, the expense of an asset to each period benefited by the asset. The cost of the asset is divided up, spread across, and charged against the accounting periods of its estimated lifetime. This allows companies to charge the expenses associated with an asset against the profits it generates during the periods in which it is used. There are many methods to calculate depreciation, such as sum of year digits, declining balance, group and composite depreciation, and straight line. For the purpose of the example used, we will focus on straight-line depreciation. The formula for straight-line depreciation is

$$D = \frac{P - SV}{n}$$

where

D = Annual depreciation

P = Initial cost of the asset

SV = Salvage values of the asset

n = Expected depreciable life of the asset.

This is a function of

- ✦ Cost of the asset
- ✦ Estimated lifetime of the asset
- ✦ Salvage value (if any) of the asset
- ✦ Method of depreciation used—straight line, Accelerated Cost Recovery Standard (ACRS), etc.

Example

Using an emergency response vehicle as an example, let's say that $10,000 is spent, we plan to keep the vehicle four years, and the salvage value is $5,000. Using the formula

$$D = \frac{P - SV}{n}$$

where

D = Annual depreciation **(unknown variable)**
P = Initial cost of the asset **($10,000)**
SV = Salvage values of the asset **($5,000)**
n = Expected depreciable life of the asset **(4)**

then

$$D = \frac{\$10,000 - \$5,000}{4}$$

D = $1,250 per year.

What is the benefit gained from performing this calculation? Well, you can illustrate to management that spending $10,000 on an emergency response vehicle now will be worth a $1,250 write-off every year for four years.

Rate of Return. The rate of return is a measure that allows comparison between two different alternatives. It is a function of the ratio of the present value of the net income generated over time by the asset divided by the cost of the asset, usually expressed as a percentage. In other words, the amount of money generated by two alternative projects is translated into something resembling an interest rate. In this manner, the company may chose which project will yield the highest return for its money. Many companies also have a minimum attractive rate of return, which is the lowest rate of return acceptable before a project will even be considered.

The formula for rate of return is

$$R = \frac{P_i - P_o}{P_o}$$

where

R = Rate of Return
P_i = Net present value of all expected inflows
P_o = Net present value of all expected outflows.

The rate of return is a function of

+ Initial cost of the asset(s)
+ Expected cash outflows, which include the cost of:
    - Safety program implementation (e.g., confined space, lockout/tagout, etc.)
    - Equipment (e.g., fire extinguishers, fire protection, etc.)
    - Training
    - New employees (e.g., safety professionals, industrial hygienists, etc.)
    - Maintenance
    - Repairs
+ Cash inflows such as cost savings or payments for goods and services and expected:
    - Workers' compensation and insurance savings
    - Decrease in overtime, productivity, turnover, training costs, etc.
    - Decrease in OSHA citations

+ Salvage value (if any) of the asset
+ Discount rate used by the company, such as
  - Minimum acceptable rate of return or
  - Cost of capital (company's borrowing costs) or
  - Rate of inflation.

Example

Building on the previous example, let's say we have a choice between two emergency response vehicles. One vehicle will cost $10,000, it has a salvage value of $5,000, and will require about $1,000 per year in maintenance. The cost of money is 15 percent interest, and we plan to keep the vehicle for four years. The alternative is a $20,000 vehicle with a salvage value of $9,000 that will require about $500 per year in maintenance. Using the formula below for each option:

$$R_1 = \frac{P_i - P_o}{P_o}$$

where

$$R_2 = \frac{P_i - P_o}{P_o}$$

where

P_i = $5,000 + $5,000

Salvage Value + Depreciation

P_i = $9,000 + $11,000

Salvage Value + Depreciation

P_o = $10,000 + $1,000

Cost + Maintenance

P_o = $20,000 + $500

Cost + Maintenance

R_1 = −0.09

R_2 = −0.02.

Why is it beneficial to be able to illustrate to your management that you can perform this calculation? Well, you can point out that, even though R_1 is cheaper than R_2, it has a worse rate of return. In the case of the negative calculation, the value closest to zero is the best option because, when considering cost inflows, salvage value and depreciation are the included values. When considering out-flows, the cost of the vehicle and forecasted annual maintenance are the included values. Expected inflows that appear to wash out as equals include worker compensation savings and insurance savings, overtime, productivity, turnover, training costs and savings, and a decrease in OSHA citations. Expected outflows that appear to wash out as equals include only training. Maintenance and repairs do not wash out and are included in the calculation. The other variables are not applicable to this particular problem.

Replacement Analysis. Replacement analysis provides an economic comparison of two asset choices, a *defender* (current asset) versus a *challenger* (asset being considered for purchase). It is commonly used when determining whether or not to replace an existing asset with a new or more efficient one, or when comparing different options for procuring equipment, such as buying or leasing. The costs and expenses associated with the assets are converted into an EUAC. This determines how much expense will be associated with a given asset in one year's time, thus providing a uniform benchmark for comparison. Once the EUAC has been determined, all the company needs to do is choose the lowest cost option. For example, to determine which is more feasible, buying or leasing a particular asset, the formulas below can be used. Here the defender formula is used to perform the purchase option and the challenger formula to calculate the lease option.

Formula for the defender: Formula for the challenger:
    (Purchase Option)   *(Lease Option)*

$$EUAC_d = P - SV + AOC \qquad EUAC_c = L + AOC$$

where   where

P = Purchase cost of the asset L = Lease cost of the asset
SV = Salvage value of the asset AOC= Annual operating cost
AOC= Annual operating cost.

This is a function of

+ Initial cost of the asset
+ Salvage value (if any) of the asset
+ Annual operating cost
+ Lease cost.

Example

Using another similar example, let's say we have the option between two emergency response vehicles. One vehicle will cost $10,000; it has a salvage value of $5,000 and will require about $1,000 per year in maintenance. The alternative is to lease an emergency response vehicle for 4 years at $2,000 per year and pay about $500 per year in maintenance. Using the formula below for each option:

Formula for the defender:

$$EUAC_d = P - SV + AOC$$

where

P = $10,000
SV = $5,000
AOC = $1,000

then

$$EUAC_d = \$10,000 - \$5,000 + \$1,000$$
$$= \$6,000.$$

Formula for the challenger:

$$EUAC_c = L + AOC$$

where

L = $2,000 x 4 years
AOC = $500

then

$$EUAC_c = \$8,000 + \$500$$
$$= \$8,500.$$

Initially, by using this formula you can illustrate the benefits of purchasing over leasing. However, you also verify the relatively low cost of purchasing this vehicle in the first place. Being able to perform this calculation illustrates to management that you have *examined all of the options*, rather than merely *indicating* that the company needs to purchase an emergency response vehicle.

Retirement Analysis. Retirement analysis is the method used to find the lowest EUAC of an asset based on the number of years it will be used. This method of analysis allows the company to decide the most economical length of time to utilize an asset. With this information, the company can decide when to replace the asset, or assign a length of time during which the asset can be most economically utilized as a factor in a replacement analysis. This allows the replacement analysis to be conducted more accurately.

Example

Let's look at the emergency vehicle based on a service life of four, five, six, seven, or eight years. Again, the formula to use is as follows:

$$EUAC_d = P - SV + AOC$$

Suppose that we have to determine how long we want to keep the emergency response vehicle. Given the following information for each year—salvage value, annual operating costs, capital recovery (CR), equivalent operating costs (EOC)—the following table can be generated for each year of use:

EUAC for n years

Years (n)	SV	AOC	CR	EOC	Total (CR + EOC)
1	$9,000	$2,500	$5,300	$2,500	$7,800
2	8,000	2,700	3,681	2,595	6,276
3	6,000	3,000	3,415	2,717	6,132
4	2,000	3,500	3,670	2,886	6,556
5	0	4,500	3,429	3,150	6,579

The result is that the minimum EUAC of $6,132 per year for the emergency response vehicle for three years indicates the remaining life of the asset. Why is it a benefit to be able to illustrate to your management that you can perform this calculation? Well, when you are trying to justify purchasing a new emergency response vehicle, this calculation could provide additional information regarding the economic value of keeping the current vehicle. It is certainly better than justifying an expense by saying, "This one sure is getting old and we need a new one." The calculations give credibility to your conclusions for needing a new emergency response vehicle.

Cost-Benefit Analysis. Cost-benefit analysis is a method used to analyze the effects of making a change in a process. Typically, cash flows of present procedures are compared against predicted cash flows incurred under the change. The advantage of using the cost-benefit analysis is the ability to monetize costs of intangibles (e.g., good will, reputation of a company, the cost of a life, cost of future injuries, decreased turnover, decreased training, etc.). The estimates used must be accompanied by realistic, conservative accounting assumptions. Without realistic assumptions to force the solution to the worst-case scenario, errors could occur which invalidate the estimate basis.

Tying the Cost to Lost-Time Accident Savings

Another way to justify the cost of your program is to tie the reduction of lost-time accidents (LTAs) to cost savings. Make sure your plant manager knows that none of this is free and cannot be done with one person. To attain that quantum leap takes—you got it—money. Let's assume that the cost of a lost-time accident is $40,000 and that recent history indicates two LTAs/year. The annual cost for the safety department is $100,000.

Tell management that, whatever the cost to get from an incident rate of 5 to 2.5, double the cost to get from 2.5 to 1.5. To get from

1.5 to 1, double that figure again. The cost increase is for equipment, staff, resources, and rewards for achieving the postulated goal. Weight the goal so that you assume the risk early on, but the company assumes more of the risk as you approach your goal. For example, if you quickly get to one year without a lost-time accident and a sustained incident rate of 2.5, the payback is 0.5 times the cost to get from 5.0 to 2.5. As you approach 1.0 that multiplier increases to 0.75, 0.85, and may rise as high as 1.0. As you can see in Table 1, the payback can increase quite rapidly.

	Goal		Cumulative Safety Department Budget	LTA Averted Cost	Cumulative LTA Averted Cost	Payback to Safety Department
IR		LTA				
2.5	1 Year without LTA		$100,000	$80,000	$80,000	0.5 x $80,000 = $40,000
1.5	2 Years without LTA		$200,000	$80,000	$160,000	0.75 x $160,000 = $120,000
1.0	3 Years without LTA		$300,000	$80,000	$240,000	0.85 x $240,000 = $204,000
0.5	4 Years without LTA		$400,000	$80,000	$320,000	1.0 x $640,000 = $320,000

Table 1. Payback from reducing the incident rate

Justifying Safety Using Sales and Profit Margins

In times of keen competition and low profit margins, safety may contribute more to profits than an organization's best salesman. It is necessary for the salesman of a business to sell an additional $1,667,000 in products to pay the costs of $50,000 in annual losses from injury, illness, damage, or theft, assuming an average profit on sales of 3 percent. The amount of sales required to pay for losses will vary with the profit margin. Table 2 below shows the dollars of sales required to pay for different amounts of costs for accident losses (i.e., if an organization's profit margin is 5%, it would have to make sales of $500,000 to pay for $25,000 worth of losses. With a 1% margin, $10,000,000 of sales would be necessary to pay for $100,000 of the costs involved with accidents).

Yearly Incident Costs	Profit Margin				
	1%	2%	3%	4%	5%
$1,000	100,000	50,000	33,000	25,000	20,000
5,000	500,000	250,000	167,000	125,000	100,000
10,000	1,000,000	500,000	333,000	250,000	200,000
25,000	2,500,000	1,250,000	833,000	625,000	500,000
50,000	5,000,000	2,500,000	1,667,000	1,250,000	1,000,000
100,000	10,000,000	5,000,000	3,333,000	2,500,000	2,000,000
150.000	15,000,000	7,500,000	5,000,000	3,750,000	3,000,000
200,000	20,000,000	10,000,000	6,666,000	5,000,000	4,000,000
SALES REQUIRED TO COVER LOSSES					

Table 2. Sales to Offset Accidents = ($Losses x 100)/Profit Margin (%)

Business Concepts for Safety Professionals Who Are Consultants

Not all safety professionals work in large corporations anymore. As downsizing has taken its toll, many safety professionals work in small businesses or have their own consulting business. Those who are consultants often don't succeed because they fail to manage their finances. This is where knowing financial management principles is imperative to survive. Safety consultants must practice *smart* financial management in order to flourish.

You don't have to be a certified public accountant (CPA) to manage your business, but you must know the basics. You should be familiar with at least the following key areas.

1. **The Financial Statement.** Your company's goal is to make money, right? Well, one way to do that is to maintain a good financial statement. It is not unlike the company diary. It is a

portfolio that contains a balance sheet, statement of cash flow, and a statement of retained earnings. It shows the way business is conducted, where profit centers are, and where potential land mines are buried. One prime mistake is thinking that you can keep track of all this in your head. You've got to have a consistent way of tracking activity, and it needs to be on paper.

Lenders look at the balance sheet to see how much your company is worth or how liquid it is. The balance sheet shows what you have—assets—versus what you owe—liabilities. Ultimately, it shows your net worth. Both assets and liabilities are described in terms of current and noncurrent items. Current items are those items that will be collected or are due within twelve months. Current assets include accounts receivable, inventory, and prepaid expenses. Noncurrent assets include property and equipment. Current liabilities include items such as payroll taxes, accounts payable, and deferred income. Noncurrent liabilities include multi-year loans and other debt commitments that stretch past a year.

Total assets minus total liabilities calculate a company's net equity or net worth. The goal is to keep the balance sheet positive rather than negative. Negative numbers mean you owe more than you own. It is not necessarily a death knell, but it should be a concern. Ideally, your debt-to-equity ratio should be no more than two to one.

2. **The Income Statement.** The income statement shows the company's bottom line as net income or net profit. A useful way to arrange income statements is in a year-to-year comparative format. The income statement lists annual net sales— gross sales minus returns and other allowances. For example, if you have net sales of $300,000, it deducts the cost of goods sold (say $160,000) from that, leaving a gross profit of $140,000.

The income statement also covers net operating income. This is the sum of your selling and administrative expenses subtracted from your gross profit. Salaries, employee benefits, rent, payroll taxes, utilities, office supplies, and costs for marketing and advertising would be subtracted from gross profit. For this example, let's assume these expenses total $97,000. When this figure is subtracted from gross profit, you have net operating income (in this case $43,000). Lastly, subtract interest income and interest expenses to arrive at a net profit before tax. If you were operating in the red, it would show up here as negative profit, or a loss.

3. **Cash-flow Analysis.** Based on the information in your balance sheet and income statement, an accountant can prepare a statement of cash flow for your company. It shows the sources and uses of cash (e.g., net borrowing under credit agreements, cash used in investing, proceeds from long-term debts, and dividends paid). It's a no-brainer that tracking the flow of money in and out of the business is fundamental to the big picture, but unless you're particularly adept with accounting terms and practices, arranging a statement of cash flow is a task best left to an accountant.

That doesn't mean that you shouldn't stay as close to the numbers as possible. Safety managers should review balance sheets once a month, and every three months or so put together a statement of changes in financial condition. That will tell you where funds are coming from and how they are being applied. It also lets you compare working capital from one period to the next.

These simple principles can assist you in tracking your costs. Perhaps they will give you the tools to turn your safety department from a cost center into a profit center. And perhaps you will attract a mentor who will spy your attention to detail and the bottom line. This could change management's perception of you from the "safety guy" to "business person." Others in the company may see that you are on the fast track while they are muddling through the day-to-day grind and wonder how you made it to the top. All this notoriety can come from merely knowing more than safety and illustrating how you track your costs and show fiduciary responsibility. Now that is a formula for success!

Conclusions

Remember, top-management commitment equals program success. Use applicable safety and health standards, use engineering, workers' compensation, and financial principles to sell your safety and health programs. Require sign-off for risk acceptance. You may even want to befriend an accountant, CPA, or the comptroller in the accounting department. That person can make your life a lot easier, especially when performing these gymnastic calculations. In any event, do your homework and calculate the *dollars and sense* of your safety and health programs. By all means, make it easy for your management to say "YES," and hard to say "NO."

As we move on, your next challenge is leadership. If you are successful in demonstrating that safety is a key business objective, chances are your company will look to you as a leader. Now you must become a leader. Accomplishing this is much harder than it appears and is fraught with many opportunities to fail. Your job is to successfuly become the leader your company is looking for, which will cement you into the company as a pillar of credibility.

On Leadership

Do You Really Want to Be a Leader?

Students sometimes think that leaders live ensconced in thoughts about the distant future; that they are surrounded by content, smiling, and appreciative people—all seeking a willing mentor; that their days are filled with thinking, studying, relaxed research of the latest trends, unchallenged respect, and endless harmony—no conflicts, no arguments. After all, if you're a leader, people listen to you. Right?

As you become more experienced in dealing with the world, you realize that leading can be awfully lonely and terribly frustrating. It can very easily make you cynical.

Today, there are more people who want to become leaders. When asked why, they really don't know, except that they think leaders get paid more money. Little do they know that, as a leader, you get handed lots of abuse. A good leader takes a little more of the blame, a little less of the credit, and does a lot more of the work.

To those interested in becoming a leader, ask yourself the following five questions:

1. **Do other people's failures annoy me or challenge me?** Every company has employees who need a lot of help. Do the failures of the people who work for you annoy you or challenge you to help them improve? Do you look for ways to help them succeed over their shortcomings? Do you encourage them to find ways to improve? If not, being a leader may not be for you.

2. **Am I using people in my interactions, or am I cultivating and mentoring them?** Simply put, do you manipulate people, or do you mentor them to be better professionals? If you are a manipulator, people will ultimately discover your devices and you will lose their loyalty. They will leave, creating a hole in your organization. They will also surely warn others of your manipulative tactics. If you are a manipulator, being a leader is not for you.

3. **Do I direct people or do I develop them?** Are you wrapped up in telling people what to do, or do you look for ways for your staff to learn from every task? Are you more concerned with the mechanics of getting things done, or are you more concerned with *why* you are doing what you are doing? Are you more concerned about a milestone that is being reached or about the benefit derived from what is being done? If you are more concerned about the mechanics, being a leader is not for you.

4. **Do I criticize or do I encourage?** Our first instinct is to criticize. Why didn't you do it this way or that way? Take every opportunity to encourage people to do things *their* way. When they fail, encourage them to try again. Remember, as a leader you are *constructing* people not *destructing* people.

If your style leans toward destructing, being a leader is not for you.

5. **Do I shun controversy or judiciously pick my battles?** There are too many managers today who avoid controversy and conflict at all costs. There are also managers who look for every opportunity to argue just to play the devil's advocate. To be a successful leader, you need to pick your battles carefully and fight them to win. You need to be prepared for controversy, but not look for controversy. If you shun controversy at all costs, being a leader is not for you.

Good leaders are definitely needed today. But it is difficult to always live in the limelight and not get a little arrogant. You need people around you who will keep you humble. The old saw is true: Power corrupts, and absolute power corrupts absolutely.

Becoming a leader requires that you surrender yourself to others. You need a good listening ear, a strong will to discipline, and the ability to undergo severe scrutiny without taking it personally. If you are very sensitive and have a thin skin, it will be very difficult for you.

Leaders face many frustrations. People will ask for your advice on what to do, and then they will not follow it. You will try to shape people and they will resist, even though the change would benefit them. You will try to show people where the land mines are, and they will step on them anyway. You will see people fail, and fail, and fail.

Are you cut out for this tiring, thankless position? You must carefully examine yourself and decide if it is worth the sacrifice. Ponder it thoughtfully. Take stock of yourself.

If you still decide that you want to be a leader, you may find your-self in front of the mirror, asking, "Am I really from this planet?"

Leaders Are from Mars, Managers Are from Venus

History has proven time and time again that governments and nations crumble for lack of leadership. Large multinational com-panies, as well as small businesses, falter for lack of leadership. So it's no wonder that safety departments fail for lack of leadership.

We all know that, no matter what the corporate title, *leaders* act and think differently from *managers*. And we know that leader-ship is important. But why should we draw a distinction between leaders and managers?

Are You a Safety "Leader" or a Safety "Manager"?

Throughout your career, you will work with and for many man-agers, but only with a few real leaders. You can learn how to lead from those who are talented trail-blazers and how not to lead from those who merely manage. I have learned from lead-ers in all aspects of my profession, including business contacts, members of professional associations, and community, state, and national figures. I have also learned how *not* to lead from individuals in these same groups.

You will see that there is a clear distinction between leaders and managers. Managers tend to be internally motivated toward their careers. They tend to be "me first" oriented. Leaders, on the other hand, tend to be externally motivated toward their own careers. They tend to be "other" oriented. Managers "get by," but leaders "have a vision." Consequently, managers tend to maintain the status quo, while leaders are champions for change.

Who Is a Manager?

My definition of a *manager* is someone who merely keeps the place from blowing up: no vision, no plan, just get me to five o'clock.

Who Is a Leader?

You are a leader if you can get someone else to do something you want him or her to do because *they* want to do it.

Qualities of a Leader

What makes a person a leader? What makes people want to follow a leader? Some of the characteristics that define a leader are described below:

1. **Motivation.** This is a key ingredient and a tool leaders use to inspire professionals to get work done. It is not just a manipulative tool, but an inherent *spirit* that a leader provides as support to team members. Motivation has three basic components: energization, direction, and feedback.

   Energization. Energization involves using a secondary drive. In short, what people hope to get from a job, a position, a career, an avocation, drives them to action. Secondary drives can include basic goals, interests, and attitudes. Once leaders discover secondary drives, they use them to help energize people to achieve the desired results.

   Direction. Once people are energized, they are ready to do something. Now they need a direction. Direction includes the why, when, where, and who for action. More explicitly, direction includes what goals are to be achieved, what products are to be generated, and how these goals and products are to be integrated and used.

   Feedback. Lastly, motivation includes feedback. Feedback reinforces behavior and allows mid-course correction, keeping goals flexible. Without feedback, performance cannot be measured effectively.

2. **Integrity.** Leaders set the example. People look to leaders to set the norm, especially in safety. Since safety managers make the rules, it is imperative they also follow them to the letter. They do not leave anything to question. If employees are unsure about what the rules are, chaos will ultimately result.

3. **Loyalty**. Leaders are loyal to their families, their company, their employees, and themselves. They make promises sparingly, but keep them faithfully. They serve the people who work for them as well as the ones for whom they work.

4. **Courage.** Leaders are brave enough to go to management and ask for resources to complete tasks. Leaders are brave enough to give credit to subordinates when credit is deserved. They take the heat when failures occur and exhibit the courage that removes obstacles and breaks down barriers to accomplishing tasks. Leaders also have the courage to make unpopular decisions. Sometimes they must make decisions when only a few, if any, colleagues agree. Many historical leaders have been in the same position. For example, what would have happened in World War II if General George Patton had taken a vote before deciding to continue the pursuit of the enemy, even though he was dangerously low on fuel? Leaders will sometimes make difficult and unpopular decisions. They must have the courage to do what they feel is *best* and not what is *expedient*. The result is that the leader will not always be liked by his followers—it goes with the territory.

5. **Good Communication.** Leaders are effective and articulate communicators. They are able to express themselves persua-

sively in group settings. They are comfortable speaking in a staff meeting, a safety meeting, a boardroom, and a training session, to small groups and large groups, and among professionals as well as lay people. They enjoy conveying their message equally in a formal presentation or an impromptu conversation. In general, leaders speak last on a subject; speak authoritatively; hold their listeners' attention; exhibit straight talk and down-to-earth attitudes; speak well extemporaneously; provide emotional links to co-workers, peers, and superiors; and exhibit strong, deep convictions.

6. **Knowledge.** Leaders are respected for their professional experience. They tend to be experts in their field and stay current with events in their profession: They know when the next proposed standard that affects their workplace is expected; they know the trends in research and the best commercial practices for their products. Usually, they are well-networked in their profession to maintain this knowledge base.

7. **Vision.** Leaders convey a vision of the future. They are the catalyst that defines the organization's mission and potential. Organizations are in search of a leader who has a plan and who is actually working that plan. People find security in an association with someone who is constantly looking ahead, someone who is willing to change to meet upcoming demands.

8. **Humility.** Leaders who are comfortable in their abilities do not boast. They understand that humility is a journey, not a destination. However, humility and meekness should not be confused with weakness. Leaders are not members of the group known as the **D**ependent **O**ver-abused **O**rganization of **R**eally **M**eek and **T**imid Souls (DOORMATS). I don't know any successful safety managers who are members of this group. DOORMATS usually are not in leadership positions for very long.

9. **Personnel Development.** Leaders understand people and their various needs in the workplace. They understand that people and their needs are different, and are able to identify what people want from a job, a position, or a career. Leaders are able to map out short- and long-term goals for their people, nurture a commitment from the group, and lead to success by example. Skills needed for personnel development are:

Developing commitment. Leaders make a direct emotional connection with fellow professionals that goes far beyond the usual boss-subordinate relationship. Leaders involve others, seek advice, ask for information, solicit solutions to problems, and provide frequent positive feedback. They get people who work for them to create solutions and take responsibility for outcomes.

Encouraging empowerment. Leaders encourage fellow professionals to be self-reliant. They delegate to other professionals and provide others with an environment for success; that is, they lower barriers and provide the tools and support necessary to succeed. They also sustain an environment with opportunities to take limited risks and to fail without fear. If professionals are frightened that they might lose their jobs, they will be tentative about initiating change. The result is that they never take chances.

Ensuring success. Many managers hire people who are less intelligent than they are, fearing that smart people may surpass them. Leaders, on the other hand, try to hire people smarter than they are. If these people succeed, leaders get credit for hiring the right people. They are always looking for their replacements because leaders understand that, in order to move up in the organization, they need to groom their successors—maybe more than one, for contingency purposes.

Inspiring lofty accomplishments. Outside the group, leaders give credit to individuals for their successes and take responsibility for the individual failures, offering no excuses. Leaders use accomplishable goals to build greater and more difficult goals and to encourage other people to do more. Each time a goal is set, they make the next level a little more difficult, constantly building to surpass previous achievements. Leaders aim for the quantum leaps rather than take the linear approach to performance improvement. They are passionate, committed, and tenacious about goal setting and accomplishment.

Modeling appropriate behavior. Leaders have earned respect because they symbolize the values and norms of the group. They lead by example: Safety managers make the rules they must follow without exception; they must also exhibit knowledge in their field.

Focusing attention on important issues. Leaders have the ability to ferret through all the facts and discover the key issues and tough problems. They recognize that only a limited number of goals can be pursued at one time, so they take care in choosing what to emphasize.

Connecting their group to the outside world. A leader serves as a link to the overall organization and the rest of the world. Leaders represent the group in the outside world, project the image of the group to the outside world, and relay information to and from the outside world. They get involved with university professors, researchers, and technologists in order to keep up with technical issues, and they keep in touch with their counterparts at other companies.

Teaching professionals the nature of leadership. Many professionals spend years in college learning about a specific discipline; but they learn little, if anything, about leadership.

I've never seen a college course on leadership. Professionals need to know that there are tools for effectively managing and effective tools for leading. Trained professionals succeed in their chosen field, get promoted as a result of this success, and suddenly find that they have few management or leadership skills. They are potentially doomed to failure, or at least mediocrity, without proper leadership training.

Putting professionals in the proper environment to learn leadership. Leaders allow their professionals to practice leadership in a positive learning environment. Just as a safety professional learns that classroom safety is far different in the real world, so must a safety professional learn how to apply hands-on leadership skills.

10. **Delegating.** It's one of the most important skills you'll ever master. Delegating doesn't mean passing off work; it means giving others authority, responsibility, and accountability. People who fail to delegate burn out early—the "Peter Principle." People who fail to delegate do not effectively match the right people with the tasks for the most efficient outcomes. No one person can try to do everything without wasting valuable resources of time, money, and morale. Steps to effective delegation include:

Trusting your staff. One fruitful approach to use when superiors question staff is, "If you don't trust the people working for you, get rid of them and hire people you do trust." The same is true with professionals. Give them the opportunity to try to succeed—or fail and learn if necessary. Let them know that honest mistakes will not be punished. Let them know that you are providing a safe environment for calculated risk taking and decision making.

Avoid seeking perfection. Engineers sometimes seek perfection at all costs. At some point, engineers must stop engineering and start implementing. This implies some amount of imperfection; however, the imperfection falls within specific acceptable boundaries. Also, over-engineering implies a continual evolution: If left to their own ends, engineers will design and design and design, never implementing, but always trying to improve the design.

Giving effective job instructions. The workplace is busy. We almost expect people to read our minds. This approach to communication predestines failure. Explicitly communicate goals and performance standards at the beginning of a project and provide frequent feedback to ensure progress.

Recognizing the talent and ability of others to complete projects. We need to understand that others approach problems differently from us. In many cases, there are numerous paths to the same solution. Be flexible and allow for variability in problem solving.

Recognizing skills. Recognize that some professionals have much stronger technical skills than leadership skills, and allow these individuals to freely develop their technical expertise.

Following up on progress. Failure to follow up is probably the most grievous error in delegating. Provide employees with clear milestones that include dates and tangible products. Require a contingency plan with priorities if milestones are not met. Follow-up here is critical. If these plans are not met, consider redelegation of the tasks.

Praising the efforts of your staff. A simple "thanks," taking employees out to lunch, a brief memo to superiors, a pat on the back, these are just small examples of how to say "thank you" for a job well done. Also, remember, praise in public, punish in private.

Avoiding reverse delegation. If an employee has accepted the work that was delegated, do not allow the employee to offer incomplete work. Provide guidance to successfully complete the work.

Don't make delegation an all-or-nothing proposition. Some employees need to build confidence a little at a time. Allow employees to do pieces that they feel comfortable with and can succeed doing to build confidence. Keep building on this base until employees feel competent in the work assigned.

Delegating to the lowest possible level. This ensures that you are making use of everyone's talents and applying your time most effectively.

What a Leader Does

When leaders arrive on the scene, what do they do? Well, one thing they do is assess the situation. They examine the OSHA 300 log, the 300A summary of work-related injuries and illnesses, and the OSHA 301 injuries and illnesses incident report. They figure out what has been happening, determine what needs fixing, and begin to plan how to correct apparent problems. They determine what programs are in place and if these programs are up to date. They assess whether accurate data is being collected and distributed. Leaders also assess the corporate culture. This assessment will provide an insight on how far the company needs to go to reach an ideal safety culture.

Once all of the examining is done, the leader formulates a plan. This takes time and effort and may require late nights during the formative stages. What does a plan consist of? Well, for one thing, a plan consists of a time frame that is long enough to show results. Personally, I live by the "five-year plan" for everything from career planning, to financial planning, to job planning. Perhaps the five-year goal may not be reached because it will change every year. You are changing it every year because you are reviewing it every year. Just writing it down and storing a plan away for future resurrection at the end of five years without revision will have defeated the purpose of planning to achieve goals.

Next, set a goal that is achievable. Is the goal a certain incident rate value? Is the goal a certain percent reduction in incident rates? Is it improved productivity? Is it linked to quality? Is it linked to engineering design improvements? Is it linked to Process Safety Management? Is it attaining VPP status? You will need to set a goal that reflects your own corporate vision and the current regulatory environment (e.g., ISO 9000). Put together steps that will need to be accomplished along with a time frame. Assess progress every year. Monthly performance reviews may be in order for critical items. Regardless, regular performance assessments must be made to ensure goal completion.

In the beginning, have a meeting with the people with whom you will be working closely. As you sit down with each person, ask questions like, "Where do you want to be in five years?" or "What do you see yourself doing in five years?" You may be surprised at some of the responses you will get. Your job as a leader is to help your team members achieve their goals. You actually work for them! Wow! What a concept! It is your job to assist those working with you to achieve their goals so they will help you achieve yours.

What Did You Conclude?

Reflecting on the qualities just outlined, are you a safety leader or a safety manager? Do people follow you because they are required to, or because they want to? The difference between a leader and a manager may be as far as Mars is from Venus, or, at the very least, reflect the difference between a job and a career. As safety professionals, we find plenty of people around telling us what we should do, but rarely do we have someone invest in our careers and help us to achieve our own goals while also achieving a common corporate goal. Good leaders inspire people to both work and enjoy working at the same time.

If you have just grown into a position where you are managing people, or you are managing people and wondering why your attrition rate is so high, perhaps considering some of the approaches we have just reviewed can help you *lead* your group rather than *manage* your group.

Followership

Everywhere you turn, young professionals want to be leaders: Fresh out of school, they want to be the boss; they want to run the department without a clue about what they're stepping into. Without career seasoning in how to accomplish safety and without the experience of how to link all the elements together in an integrated fashion, asking to lead is asking for failure. In order to be a good leader, you must first be a good follower. No leader worth his or her salt would ever accept a replacement who has not demonstrated good *followership*.

Mastering followership is not easy and takes time. Many in the industry call it "paying your dues." The *dues* refer to the requisite experience and mistake-making that season you to clear the hurdles that will be thrown in front of you and your department. Without experience as a good follower, you are doomed to failure in the role of leader.

If you have cleared the hurdles and head your department, when you interview new candidates you need to structure questions that assess their followership characteristics. The following list summarizes those characteristics.

A good follower:

1. **Has unselfish humility.** When you are asked to do a task that appears to be beneath you, do it without complaining and whining. You may not realize the importance of such a task until later. Too many professionals today want to sit in an office and tell everyone what to do. When you are a follower, your job is to suck it up and do the menial tasks. Who knows, it may make your boss and your department look better just when they need the image enhancement.

2. **Gives unconditional commitment.** Today, there is little commitment, let alone *unconditional* commitment to your department. Much of industry has brought this on itself through downsizing, rightsizing, and sometimes capsizing. Without commitment to your boss and department, you may fail to come through just when they need you the most. Without unconditional commitment, you are doomed to mediocrity—your career growth will be severely stunted.

3. **Is obedient.** When you are told to do something at a crucial moment, don't question to the nth degree. By the time you get an adequate answer, the whole facility might be burned down. Just say, "Yes, sir," or "Yes, ma'am," and ask questions later. If you argue with superiors, this can easily be construed as insubordination. Your boss might feel the need to relieve you during emergencies, replacing you with someone who is cooperative. If you can't master obedience, there is no place for you. If you are not obedient, your future in the business world may be a short one.

4. **Anticipates difficulty.** When you are asked to take a task to completion, assume that there will be problems. Schedule with some slack for delays. Anticipate that not all information will be readily available. Be ready to persevere and work a longer

than eight-hour day. Prepare a Plan B, Plan C, even a Plan D, in case Plan A falters. In other words, plan for the worst and hope for the best. Then you won't be surprised when things begin to unravel—you'll have contingency plans to handle it.

5. **Demonstrates initiative.** How many professionals have you seen who have to be told what to do, down to the minutest detail? And if you don't tell them, they complain, "You didn't say I had to do that!" Take the initiative; do things that you haven't been told. If you have aspirations to be a future leader, initiative is a key ingredient. How many leaders do you know who sat on their hands waiting for someone else to tell them what to do?

6. **Knows the priorities.** A college professor once approached a student to sign up for a robotics class he would be teaching. He claimed it would be very interesting. The student replied, "I could spend my life taking *interesting* classes. But I want to graduate on time." The student had set a priority not to deviate from the degree plan, regardless of how interesting other classes looked. In the working world you must always set priorities and *only* alter them when your superiors redirect you with their priorities. This will ensure successful projects, as well as show your superiors that you recognize and implement their priorities, regardless of your own.

7. **Displays Loyalty.** Have we seen the last of loyalty? Is everyone out to stab his or her boss in the back to get promoted? When someone attacks your boss or your department, be the first to come to the aid of your boss and your colleagues. When your boss needs your help, give it willingly.

8. **Has a thankful heart.** Too many professionals look around at what everyone else has and wonder "Why don't I have that? I want what they have!" Well, remember, generally those who

have more responsibility have earned it. You, too, must earn your way. Be thankful for what you have at each stage of your career.

9. **Is persistent.** I can't tell you how many professionals, making good money, come to me and say, "I couldn't do what you asked me because . . ." Every little hurdle seems a mile high to them. Instead of trying to find another way to do it they say, "Okay, I tried once and it didn't work, so now tell me how to do it." I remember getting a call from the site safety manager at a plant at two in the morning. He asked, "A guy got hurt, what do I do?" It wasn't serious, so I said, "What do you think you need to do?" After getting over the attitude that I was supposed to tell him how to do everything, he worked it out with my assistance. I ended the conversation by saying, "Next time, I want you to figure this all out first. When you call me, you will have several options coupled with what you did, and I will advise you accordingly." That is persistence.

10. **Completes the task.** Related to persistence is completing the task. Too many professionals today accomplish 90 percent of the task and assume someone else is going to finish it. They say, "Well, I did *most* of it." And they have no problem with that. As a professional, you were hired to complete tasks that are given to you, not *mostly complete* tasks. You should make your boss' job easier, not harder. If you always make it harder, you may wake up to find yourself fired, replaced by someone who *will* make your boss' job easier.

These are the characteristics that build followership. If you master these, over time you may be viewed as paying your dues and ready to be dubbed a leader. But remember, even at the next level, you will always have a boss, and he or she is the leader and you are the follower. No matter where you go, unless you are the CEO, you will always have some follower tasks. So keep them in mind as you scale the corporate ladder and move up the food chain. Who knows how far you might go!

The Lost Art of Faithfulness

Several years ago, at a company where I worked, I struck an agreement with the president. If an agreed-upon incidence rate could be reached, the president would carve out a corporate safety manager slot for me where none existed previously.

During this time, the industry was growing rapidly and all kinds of professionals were changing jobs at a blinding pace. In an average week, I would receive at least one phone call from a headhunter tossing out the bait, "Do you know anyone who would be interested in this job?" I would say to myself, "YES, me!" and then reply, "I know of several who are looking," and then I would offer names and phone numbers.

It would have been easy to forego my commitment during this time, going to the highest bidder. The jobs all sounded better, and seemed to offer more prestige, more status, and sometimes more money. But I had a sense of faithfulness to my commitment to the president of the company. I stuck it out. During this time I developed several close relationships with co-workers, and we were able to achieve and surpass the agreed-upon goals set with the president. Five years later, I can look back at the success the program achieved and the growth of co-workers during the process. My work was done in good conscience, and I avoided feeling guilty about leaving before I accomplished the goals I had promised to pursue.

Faithfulness is a valuable virtue in a professional. It means you can be counted on. Make promises cautiously, but keep them faithfully. It is easy to jump ship in the middle of a job when someone offers you more money, but we are not in this business just for the money. We are here to protect people, property, and the environment.

People who make great contributions to safety (or any field for that matter), who rise to the top of their professions, and enjoy success and fame, aren't simply gifted or fortunate. Instead, they intuitively reach deep within themselves for resources. They harness and effectively use qualities that we all have. One of those qualities is faithfulness to a commitment.

Here are some of the attributes of faithfulness:

1. **Practice the three "Ds."** Although many jobs aren't glamorous or don't pay well, you can add dignity, respect, and meaning to them by applying the three "Ds": diligence, dependability, and discipline.

   Diligence means that, when you are given a task, you are industrious in finding ways around the barriers, unflagging in spending all the time required to accomplish the task, and unrelenting in focusing on the details necessary to complete it.

   Dependability means that, when you are asked to do something, you can be counted on to complete the task, no matter what the obstacles. When you exhibit this quality, people respond to you positively; they are confident rather than skeptical of the job's completion.

   Discipline refers to the process of following a proven methodology to complete the tasks allocated to ensure the quality of the results. Investigate all of the factors that can affect your results and control them to the best of your ability so that your outcome is relatively unaffected by outliers.

2. **Exercise persistence.** In business and in life, persistence is the force ensuring survival and success. Too many people are guilty of premature defeat. They quit too quickly. Live by the principle "It's always too soon to quit." Too often, when people experience a setback or an emotional blow, they give up on themselves. Rather than remain faithful to themselves, their dreams and aspirations, they resign themselves to defeat. They place a maudlin emphasis on what was lost, instead of fueling a passionate desire for what can be gained. To them, the cup is half empty—or even upside down—rather than half full. In doing this, they often become crusty, stodgy, and overly cynical, and focus on the failure rather than the lessons learned. On the other hand, victory and satisfaction belong to those who don't choose the path of least resistance when faced with major life challenges.

3. **Support others when they are down.** Instead of kicking others when they are down, lift them up and offer assistance. Let them know that there is always another day to rectify the error. Reaching out to individuals facing personal or professional problems greatly improves your own chances of success.

    People remember that when they were down you helped them. There was a colleague who was fired-up to take the CSP exam. When he learned he had not passed the exam the first time through, he was very dejected. Interestingly, he only failed by a few points and should have been encouraged to take the exam again.

He told me over a cup of coffee that he had never flunked anything before! I told him, empathetically, that I had flunked the exam on my first try, and that I just got right back in the saddle and worked to pass it the next time. I also reaffirmed that his abilities were strong, and that he should be confident he would pass the next time around. He was energized to get back in the game and take the test. He passed the exam on his second attempt.

Showing empathy can have a positive impact on people. As John Eyeberg once said, "Sympathizers are spectators; empathizers wear game shoes."

4. **Think like an optimist.** John Milton wrote, "The mind is its own place, and in itself can make a heaven of hell, a hell of heaven." Believe it or not, how and what we think can actually shape our destiny. This is often called self-fulfilling prophecy.

   How many of you have ever attempted to put on a seminar or a one- or two-day conference? You put together a committee and off you go. Invariably, there is at least one "doubting Thomas" who can only agree to one thing—the conference will fail. He continually attacks the mission of the committee, trying to keep the committee from moving forward. Late in the process, the doubting Thomas says, "Why don't we change from our previously decided topic to behavior-based safety?" The retort comes, "We've been gearing up to play football, and now you want to play baseball, this late in the game?" Thankfully, this silenced the nay-sayer, however briefly.

   The lesson is clear: Turn your thinking to be more optimistic. That way you can use your mind as a lifesaving, creative tool rather than as a self-destructive weapon.

5. Tell yourself often, "Focus on the goal, not on the obstacles."

Make the choice to believe in yourself. Choose:

to be a victor, not a victim;

to soar, not sink;

to overcome, not be overwhelmed.

People who believe in themselves often can accomplish what appears to be impossible. Colleagues and superiors may even tell you a task is impossible. Say to them, "Just give me the opportunity to fail." They will be surprised when you persevere and prevail. As Sam Ewing said, "Nothing is so embarrassing as seeing someone do something you said couldn't be done."

A story of four U.S. soldiers during the Vietnam War illustrates this truth. The soldiers were riding in a jeep through a narrow path in the jungle when enemy fire suddenly erupted all around them. They stopped the jeep and jumped for cover in the jungle. As the bullets whistled overhead, the sergeant explained their three chances for survival.

"The first option is to run back onto the road, jump into the jeep, and drive straight on, but we'll be driving right into the enemy fire. Our second choice is to try escaping through the jungle, but that can also be extremely dangerous. The third thing we can do is run to the road, each of us pick up a corner of the jeep, turn it around, get in, and drive back to safety. That seems like the safest course, and I think it's our only chance."

Because jeeps are heavy military vehicles, the sergeant added, "Before we attempt this, I want to make sure each of you believes we can do it." When each soldier assured the sergeant it could be done, he ordered them to scramble back to the jeep. Each man picked up a corner of the vehicle and they turned it around. Immediately they jumped into the jeep and drove off at top speed, back to safety.

That's not the end of the story, though. When the soldiers returned to camp, no one believed they had lifted and turned the jeep. They were challenged to repeat the feat in front of everyone on the parade ground. Bets were placed, and although the soldiers wanted to prove they weren't lying, they couldn't lift the jeep. The difference was the soldiers were no longer in danger. In the jungle, they had to believe in themselves to survive. However, at the base camp, they were out of danger and their strong belief faded.

Lastly, if you take a tumble and feel like a failure, remember the words of Ralph Waldo Emerson: "Our greatest glory consists not in never falling, but in rising every time we fall."

Conclusions

First and foremost, stay faithful to yourself. Be diligent, dependable, and disciplined. Be persistent and don't quit too quickly. Show others empathy when they are down. Be optimistic rather than pessimistic.

Where Has All the Discipline Gone?

There are so many articles on coaching, facilitating, empowering, positive outcomes, emotional intelligence, trusting, alliance building, yada, yada, yada, that I *almost* buy it. With all this warm and fuzzy, "we are the world" feeling approach to safety, I have to ask, "Whatever happened to the old-fashioned, classical approach to safety, like *discipline*?"

When people do things that they aren't supposed to do, they could get hurt or killed, they could hurt others, they could blow up the facility. As safety professionals, are we merely supposed to say, "Oh my goodness! We must not have endeared trust"? Or, "Let's retrain them so that this doesn't happen again"? Or, "Poor victims, I feel your pain"?

Nonsense!

Generally speaking, people neglect things they are supposed to do for their own safety for a variety of reasons—not because safety professionals are not trusting, caring, emotionally intelligent, loving team-builders. In many cases, their carelessness stems from a *lack of discipline*. Yes, one of those "D" words.

Why Discipline?
Discipline has gotten a bad rap from many people in our society today: both from the administrators of discipline and the receivers of discipline. The administrator thinks, "I don't want to hurt someone's feelings, so I won't discipline." The receiver thinks, "Whatever I did must not be very harmful because I didn't get disciplined." As a result, the line between black and white, acceptable and unacceptable behavior, becomes gray. This creates more problems because, as human nature has proven time and time again, people will push the limits until . . . they get hurt.

What is it about discipline that makes it seem so awful? Examined up close, it's really *not* that bad. So, before we go any further, let's define discipline.

Webster's definition of discipline is: Training that is expected to produce a specific character or pattern of behavior, especially training that produces moral or mental development.

My definition of discipline is: A process of training and learning that fosters moral development.

Lately, the authoritarian approach is out of vogue and we're experiencing a resurgence of the permissive approach. In black and white terms, the authoritarian approach assumes human nature is inherently bad, while the permissive approach assumes human nature is inherently good. The permissive approach encourages the propensity for rebellious autonomy—the attitude that everything is okay until it actually hurts me. Remember the phrase, "If it feels good, do it"? People have gotten fatal illnesses as a result of this attitude. In the workplace, people can also die as a result of injury or illness because of this attitude.

The authoritarian approach teaches, among other things, personal responsibility and self-control. Look around today. We live in a society where nothing is our own fault—witness the litigious frenzy in our courts today.

Discipline does not *always* mean something bad. In fact, there are two sides to discipline, one positive and one negative. The essential principles of discipline include methods of encouragement and correction. Encouragement is the positive side of discipline and includes everything we do as safety professionals that motivates employees to do those things that constitute safe behavior.

Encouragement includes:

1. **Affirmation or verbal praise.** While walking around the facility you see someone wearing safety glasses or wearing earplugs, as required for a particular task. You approach the employee and tell him, "Hey Joe, I'm really glad to see you wearing your safety glasses (or earplugs). It sets a really good example for everyone around you!" Aside from making the employee feel good (sounds kind of warm and fuzzy), the employee will be less likely to disappoint you by not following this or some other safety rule after you have praised him. It is best to link encouragement with a specific activity, like wearing PPE. It is most effective when given unexpectedly.

2. **Goal incentives.** This is not the same as the incentive approach to safety. The goal incentives I'm referring to include activities like conducting monthly safety meetings, filing incident reports within twenty-four hours, correcting unsafe acts and conditions, checking fire protection equipment weekly, and others. They can be used to motivate employees. And, at the end of the year, supervisors can be evaluated for these activities based on the percentage completed, not on an incident rate or lost-time accidents.

   Make the supervisors responsible for conducting these activities, and accountable for getting them done. Make it clear that if any of these elements are missing, the whole system is jeopardized.

Correction, on the other hand, is the negative side of discipline. The part no one wants to get involved in. However, safety professionals must realize and live with the fact that it is difficult to enforce safety rules if you are everybody's friend. Truthfully, popularity is not our goal as safety professionals. If the employees like us, that's a bonus. But correcting unsafe behavior is far more important.

Correction includes:

1. **Verbal reproof.** Verbal reproof is an admonishment, or a warning. When employees violate the standard (rules), verbal reproof is an encouragement to be responsible. It is okay to forgive the employee for the unsafe act, but they must still be accountable and be punished. Please remember that the punishment must match the offense. If the punishment doesn't match the offense you will create ill will and an us-versus-them culture. Completing this task involves documenting the event in case the employee pushes the limit. By the way, line supervision and management, not safety, must do this.

2. **Natural consequences.** Defiant acts against the rules sometimes cause their own pain. For example, not wearing your goggles while breaking a line can mean getting sprayed in the face with caustic, causing facial burns as a natural consequence. The bottom line holds: The worker was not doing something he or she was supposed to do. Once again, supervision or management must follow through by documenting the event and administering discipline.

3. **Isolation, restrictions, and loss of privileges.** Take away the privilege of social contact. For instance, let's say you are conducting safety meetings and you have a particularly disruptive employee. What do you do? After the safety meeting, you call the person aside and inform them that they are to fulfill their monthly safety training alone, without the group. This discipline actually addresses all three of these attributes. First, the person is isolated from the other employees, thereby removing the source of disruption. Second, it restricts the employee from having interaction with other employees during the safety meetings. And third, it is a loss of the privilege of social interaction with fellow employees.

4. **Chastisement.** To correct consistent bad behavior or rebellious activities, admonish the offender. Let's say that the disruptive employee continues to be rebellious when brought back into the monthly safety meetings after isolation. This is when line management should implement chastisement, if it hasn't already. Follow the principle of punishing in private to preserve the employee's dignity. As safety professionals, we are bound not to talk about others in front of employees. However, some individuals may wish to seek consolation from fellow employees. If they choose to tell others, it is their prerogative.

The goal in all of this is to achieve worker compliance via personal responsibility, to salvage the employee, and also to document the situation in case action needs to be taken now or in the future.

In summary, here is a good model for safety professionals to persuade line management and supervision to implement:

Level 1: Verbal admonishment. Document.
Level 2: Verbal admonishment with action. Document.
Level 3: Consequential punishment. Strike three, you're out. Document.

This model is not meant to demonstrate power over employees, but rather to implement authority. It also makes employees accountable for their own actions. It's okay to forgive penitent employees for laxity, but they still must pay the price for a wrongful or unsafe act.

At its heart, this model will help motivate employees to perform safely—that is our goal.

But I Can't Fire Employees! Can I?

With all the downsizing occurring through the years, employees are getting laid off for less offensive reasons than not performing their jobs safely. Even so, it still appears that companies are afraid to discipline employees for a variety of reasons. One reason is that they want to be the employee's friend. Well, guess what? If you got into safety because of the friends you thought you'd have, you got in for the wrong reason. I would guess that, if you got into safety to make friends, by now you are extremely frustrated. I highly recommend you find another profession.

Yes, You Can Fire Employees

Another reason companies are afraid to discipline is that they are afraid of firing a valuable employee. They say, "We can't fire Joe, he's our best widget-maker." If you don't think that you can afford to fire Joe, try this test:

> *Step one,* fill a bucket half full of water.
> *Step one,* bring Joe into your office and ask him to put his hand into the bucket of water.
> *Step three,* ask Joe to remove his hand from the bucket.
> *Step four,* look in the bucket. If there is a hole in the middle where the employee had his hand, *don't fire the employee!* If there is no hole in the bucket, Joe can be replaced.

My point is this (read carefully now): Everyone—and I mean everyone—is expendable. There are no exceptions to this rule. What does this mean for safety professionals and management? They have to be willing to fire their best employee for breaking safety rules.

Breaking a human resources rule can have varying degrees of effect. If someone is caught using drugs, he or she can enter the Employee Assistance Program (EAP) and survive. Even here, if the program is not administered properly, the workplace can end up *not* a drug-free workplace but a work-free drug place. However, breaking a safety rule can result in the injury, illness, or death of one or more employees. It simply cannot be tolerated.

If you allow three violations of a lockout/tagout rule, you may have three deaths at the lockout/tagout site. Then you realize that, as safety professionals, we are here to:

Protect **YOU**
From **YOU**
In Spite of **YOU**.

The goal is to bring offenders back into line. However, if employees continually break safety rules, our job as safety professionals is to find a way to discipline them or—if required—fire them *before* they hurt themselves or others and then blame the company for their unsafe behavior.

Yet another reason companies are afraid to discipline is that they fear damaging trust between the employees and management. Trust, however, is a two-way street. Employees must feel that they can trust you and you must feel that you can trust them. I've seen company policies that give away the farm. I call this giving the inmates keys to the asylum.

Yet another challenge to discipline stems from the rebuttal, "Why punish me for something someone else did?" This is where the military viewpoint can be applied. In the armed services, when an insubordinate soldier causes pain for everyone else—like the troop running twenty miles in the rain at the crack of dawn—the other soldiers take care of business. When they do this, other good things happen. In the heat of battle, they are often drawn closer as a cohesive team. When the same realignment occurs in the workplace, good things happen there as well: things like shifts pulling together as a team or taking pride in the accomplishment of not having any safety incidents. Most importantly, it lets everyone know that unsafe behavior is unacceptable. Remember, the workplace is not a playground, it is a proving ground.

How to Walk the Walk

Aristotle once suggested: "Moral excellence comes about as a result of habit. We become just by doing just acts, temperate by doing temperate acts, and brave by doing brave acts."

Shaping employees through discipline takes someone with a strong personality—a leader. It takes someone who does not have a fragile ego or tentative self-image. So, wake up, smell the coffee, and welcome to the real world of cold hard facts! Companies want you to keep people from getting hurt, to keep people productive.

This assumes that you, as the safety professional, talk the talk and walk the walk. If you are a "Do as I say, not as I do" manager, if you don't lead by example, you will not succeed. Further, if you are not out there getting your hands dirty, trying to fix every problem you can, it will be difficult to reach that goal. An arm-chair safety professional will find it hard to get anything done, much less implement discipline.

But, if you are committed to the company and the safety process, run a tight ship, and implement discipline in the workplace, you can and will have fewer accidents, and you will further your career. You will be respected for your professionalism.

I recall an instance when a safety director sat down to talk with an employee who said, "You sure are tough. I wish you were my friend."

The director's reply was rather harsh: "The company didn't hire me to be your friend. This is not a buddy-get-a-buddy safety program. You need to realize something right now. I will never be your fishing buddy, your hunting pal, or a member of your country club. If I become your friend, and you break a safety rule, and I treat you differently than I would others, it will have defeated the whole purpose of my being here. I must maintain a separation between you and me. That separation is much like a parent-child or a student-teacher relationship. What I want is your respect. I cannot afford to be just liked. If you like me, that is okay, but it is not a requirement or a goal."

Conclusions

We need to remind ourselves that rules in our facilities are there for a reason—to protect employees from hurting themselves or others. These rules are not unlike the laws in our society. We are required by the rules of society not to steal, not to speed, not to kill. Our laws protect and stabilize the greater whole of society. Without these laws, or the enforcement of them, there is chaos.

No one promised us that everyone would like us either at work or in the real world. When you lead and implement discipline, it does not mean that you have friends all around you. You have to make hard decisions, decisions that not everyone will like. That's why you get the big bucks! This may not seem politically correct or emotionally intelligent, but, believe me, it works.

Volume Control: To Communicate Better, Reduce the Noise

Blah, blah, blah. Yada, yada, yada. Wherever you turn, somebody is talking at you: television talk shows, radio call-ins, computer chat rooms, face-to-face meetings, e-mail and voice mail, cell phones, pagers—they all produce more input than anyone can possibly absorb. And even if you could manage the deluge, would you hear anything of substance?

We are in an age of overstimulation: too much data, from too many sources, coming at us too frequently. Just trying to keep up with it all is so time-consuming we are led away from issues of substance. Yet, with a few straightforward adjustments, you can bring greater clarity and depth to your business communications.

Become a Little Hard of Hearing

Just because someone else feels like talking doesn't mean you have to listen. Be selective about whom and what you listen to, and where, when, and why you lend your ears. For example, if someone is a chronic complainer, simply avoid him or her. If a person doesn't usually get facts straight, be very cautious about listening to the input. If someone likes to hear himself talk and doesn't know how to end a sentence (I once clocked someone talking for 20 minutes without a break), cut your exposure to a minute. Be prepared to disengage yourself with a statement like, "That's interesting, but I do have to go."

Keep in mind that if you don't let something in, you don't have to deal with it. Out of the plethora of stuff coming at you, the trick is to let in messages of substance and prevent the superficial from taxing your brain.

When You Do Listen, Listen Well

We listen at about 25 percent of our capacity. Our brains process information four times faster than we can express it. I know people who talk at 56K baud and think at 28.8K baud. This creates a lot of mental dead-time while we're listening to someone speak. We fill in the time with self-talk, conversing with ourselves about what the person is saying. In effect we're always listening to two (or more) people speaking at once.

You can improve your listening skills by clearing your head of self-talk. Then focus on the person speaking, asking questions only for clarification ("Did you say 30 or 300 people were killed?"). Check to make sure their nonverbal cues—the expression in their eyes, what they're doing with their hands, etc.—are in sync with their words. For example, if their nonverbal behavior shows that they're upset, but their words deny that anything is wrong, listen to the nonverbals. That's the *real* communication.

Astute listeners often can *hear* more than a speaker is able to express in words.

Practice Verbal Self-Restraint

You can help reduce this noise pollution by communicating less and to fewer people. With today's technology it's so easy to send messages to anyone, anywhere, anytime, that we somehow believe we should do it to be effective. A recent Gallup poll shows the average Fortune 1000 worker receives 83 messages a day (electronic, voice, and written). Such volume must certainly lead to ineffectiveness.

Cut down on what you send out. Before you communicate anything, reevaluate its importance. Ask yourself, on a scale of zero to 10, how important it is for this person to get your message. If it doesn't rank as high as seven or above, forget it. You'll be surprised how few people really need your communications. CEO Charles Wang of Computer Associates has mandated that all employees practice his own version of self-restraint: He has ordered the company's e-mail system shut down for a two-hour period each day.

Promote Substantive Conversation

Why is it so rare for business people to talk about the substantive things that mean so much to us personally? Is courage too elusive a topic except for safety conferences? Is humility too intangible a concept? Why don't we talk about subjects like integrity, perseverance, faith, and responsibility?

Maybe it's time to humanize the workplace, to turn inward and learn more about our interior life. Then we can discuss with others concepts like these and the impact they have on business success. It's not necessary to wait for a management retreat to raise issues like caring, thoughtfulness, and hope. It can be done at work, if you take the time. Ask yourself: If someone did an audit of your daily communication, how much of it would be consequential? Do people remember their conversations with you? Does it make a difference to them? You can raise the quality of business conversation by becoming a communicator of substance. In turbulent times, we don't need *more* communication, we need *better* communication. Follow these approaches and you'll add a lot more substance to your business life.

Another key to demonstrating leadership is how you conduct yourself in meetings. Meetings require savvy, persuasion, and diplomacy. If you are successful in becoming a leader, you will naturally be expected to be a good communicator in meetings. The next chapter presents some tried and true techniques in mastering these meetings to ensure your success.

Meetings and Presentations

Distinguishing Remarks

Some people just like to hear themselves talk. They think they are articulate, but confuse length with quality. You hear groans and sighs from the audience after a long-winded opening. Midway through their speech, all you want is for them to "shut up." They have lost their effectiveness, and you and others tune them out. The result is that their message is diluted. They may be distinguished speakers, but for the wrong reasons.

If, on the other hand, a person articulates with a critical mass of words, their message can be delivered effectively and with elegance. It has often been said that the best solution is the simplest. The same is true when speaking: Keep it simple and to the point. Speakers who do this are distinguished for the right reasons.

One of the most powerful weapons in your professional arsenal is the ability to communicate, especially in today's information-intensive business environment. That ability is especially useful when it comes to presentations. Whether you're presenting to co-workers, employees, customers, or colleagues, you need to get your message across quickly, clearly, and effectively.

Ten strategies that can assist you in communicating effectively follow. They are culled from many years of listening to speeches and evaluating my own.

1. **Say what you mean.** Many presentations are filled with jargon, acronyms, and arcane words. Take them out of your speech and talk "people talk." Work to remove all audible pauses: the, "uhs, ums," and "ers," as well as the filler phrases like "if you will," "suffice it to say," and, "as you all know." These are clear detractors and can be quite annoying. Have you ever tried to count the number of "uhs" in someone's presentation? It can make you want to scream. Also, take out qualifying words like, "I think," "I feel," "perhaps," and "maybe." They rob your presentation of vitality and strength. There is nothing wrong with silence when you are thinking of what to say next. Pregnant pauses can make your presentation more effective and in some cases more profound.

2. **Begin with the end in mind.** Design your presentation from back to front. Begin by asking yourself "What will be different if I'm successful? What will change? What actions will be taken? How can what I say energize the listener?" Define your outcome first, and then organize your presentation to achieve that outcome. Anchor your talk and assemble your information based on the listener's need to know, not your need to talk. Remember, a good presentation is not merely an unloading or data dump; it is a means to achieve a specific outcome.

3. **Use gestures and voice inflection.** Rehearse your speech to ensure that your voice matches the emphasis of what you are speaking about and your gestures augment the message.

If you speak in a monotone you will quickly lose your audience. No matter how important what you have to say is, the bulk of what people take away is the *impression* of what you meant. Paradoxically, this impression is predominantly formed through your use of voice inflection and gestures. Make sure that your intention, voice inflection, and gestures are working in harmony to help you achieve your outcome. You don't want to overwhelm or underwhelm your audience, but you certainly want them to get your message.

4. **Get to the point.** There is no question that we live in a world where people have decreasing attention spans. We can barely sit through a 45-minute presentation where the punch line, if there is one, comes at the 44-minute mark. You sometimes wonder if the speaker even knows what point he or she is trying to make.

   The value of time puts enormous pressure on the presenter to get the point across quickly and to make sure that the listeners know what to expect. Assuming that you have met the challenge of defining your presentation's outcome, the next challenge is to create an opening that immediately sets the tone and direction of your presentation and grabs the listener's attention. A good "gotcha" opening, then, should tell listeners what's in it for them right up front. Creating such an opening takes time, creativity, and the willingness to take a risk.

5. **Edit! Edit! Edit!** This is similar to the real estate agent saying: "Location! Location! Location!" Again, remember that a good presentation is anchored in the listener's need to know, not your need to talk. Edit your speech for content and length. Your visuals should also be edited—not just the quantity, but the content as well. Each slide should display no more than twenty-five words. Good visuals are not a script for

you: Speak to your slides, don't read them. They should provide a guide to your listeners, not convey everything you want to say. Prepare yourself to present everything, if listeners ask for it; but, in fact, present very selectively.

6. **Be consistent.** Whether they know it or not, people need to hear the same messages over and over again. Your themes should be woven throughout your presentation. Those messages must be consistent in tone as well as intent if you are to be believed over the long haul. The tone of a message is not expressed solely through the words you use, but also by *how* you say them. If you have an upbeat and positive message to deliver, make sure that your voice inflection, gestures, and facial expressions are working to help you express it.

7. **Take it with you.** Communication doesn't end when you step off the podium. Your actions and attitudes will be carefully observed and measured by all who were present to hear you speak. Make sure you continue to be true to the message you delivered on stage. Don't let an insignificant aside destroy what you worked hard to create. Remember "talk the talk and walk the walk"? You had better be doing as you say to do or your listeners will see right through you—and your message will be rendered ineffective.

8. **Show enthusiasm.** Every presentation is an opportunity to advance yourself, your ideas, or your company. If you aren't enthusiastic, why should anyone else be? Creating the right message, assembling the appropriate information, and choosing the right words are critical to success, but they are not enough. You must breathe life into your words and your information.

Too many presentations are like information downloading; they lack passion and life. As a result, they often fail to really move people to action. Don't let that happen to you. Put your body, your mind, and your spirit into the message. People will choose to follow because you have touched them. Reach out to them with your emotions, and let your words live through you.

9. **Mean what you say.** Credibility is as much a function of perception as it is a fact. No two audiences are alike. They come to hear you with different needs, concerns, and agendas. Try to recognize where they're coming from and address their needs in your talk. When your listeners begin to feel that you understand them, you'll have gone a long way toward building your credibility.

10. **Make eye contact.** People respond to those who engage them, and we do that best with our eyes. Scan the audience for understanding, agreement, and attention. The most compelling messages are delivered when you consistently look into the eyes of your listeners. Eyes are the windows of the soul. You can look someone in the eye and tell if they are telling the truth or lying, are honest or dishonest. Eye contact is an especially powerful tool when you are under pressure. You can use it to engage people, focus thinking, raise credibility, and release energy.

Every time you prepare a speech, keep in mind that you are only as good as your last presentation. When you stand in front of people, you want them to remember how good your last presentation was and be excited about this one. You don't want them dreading your presentation and faking a beeper call to check out. It may be a lot of work, but good preparation is well worth its rewards—one of those is a genuine, heartfelt invitation to speak again.

In all professional situations, to distinguish yourself, you need to take control of each facet of your communication style: your words, your voice inflection, and your gestures. That's how you can influence people to understand, believe, and remember what you say. And that, of course, is your goal.

Choosing the Right Words

Speaking like a leader requires you to think before you speak. It requires striking a delicate balance: If you speak with words no one understands, no one will know what you are talking about; but if you use *only* very simple words, your speech will be imprecise, uninteresting, and unsophisticated.

"Put up with" or "tolerate," "risk" or "jeopardize," "prove" or "substantiate," "worried" or "apprehensive"—when speaking, which one of these words would *you* choose? The very simple one or the more articulate one? If you chose the simple one, it may explain why your safety meetings are boring the employees. If you chose the articulate one, it may explain why employees appear more attentive. As safety professionals, we must do our best to make our speech lively, entertaining, and articulate.

Today's English language has more synonyms than any language in the world. Given the enormous choice of words, how do we know which ones to use? By looking at the speech patterns of articulate leaders, we can draw conclusions regarding which words to use and create a simple system illustrating the *least* and *most* desirable words to use.

The Leader's Vocabulary

Leaders mix more sophisticated words with simple expressions to balance their speech. They also use commonly understood words that are *not* commonly spoken but are more authoritative and more precise.

Listen to leaders and politicians speak; they are in positions that require great skill in influencing and guiding others. They choose their words carefully. As a result, they are perceived as able communicators.

Using More Articulate Words

If you keep it too simple, your vocabulary will eventually deteriorate to a childlike, unsophisticated level and lose its effectiveness. For example, the Thesaurus lists fifty meanings for the word "get" and more than twenty-five for the word "thing." Here are a few ways these words can be used:

Get: Did the safety manager *get* (purchase) the new fire truck? We *got* (arrived) at the scene of the fire at 10:15 P.M. I *got* (received) the e-mail yesterday. The industrial hygienist *got* (obtained) the monitoring data. Did the plant manager *get* (understand) what I meant?

Thing: I need to discuss two *things* (budget items) with you. Let's clarify this *thing* (issue) before it becomes a problem. We have three *things* (topics) to discuss during the safety meeting.

It is easy to see which word adds more meaning to the statements above. They hit the mark, but don't overshoot and become esoteric.

The Importance of a Good Vocabulary

The key reason for having well-developed, spoken vocabulary skills is *not to impress* others. Rather, it is *to influence* others, either in a public setting or a private meeting. Having a good vocabulary allows us to express our ideas more persuasively. The more articulate we are, the more credible we become. By becoming more credible, our ability to influence others increases. So, if you're after a meatier budget for next year, beef up your vocabulary.

Whether you're trying to convince your company president to give your department an extra $100,000 or convince Joe Operator to follow the lockout/tagout rules, a well-developed vocabulary is important in influencing others to heed your request. And whether you are presenting at a conference or at a chapter meeting, using articulate vocabulary can mean the difference between holding your listeners' attention and looking out at a sea of heads nodding off.

Running a Good Meeting: Being a Toastmaster

Yes, you as the chapter president are the toastmaster at your meetings. The toastmaster is pivotal to the success of the meeting. Only through proper advance planning can this assignment be carried out effectively.

The primary duty of the toastmaster is to ensure a well-run meeting and to act as a genial host to smooth the transition between program participants and functionaries.

Before the Meeting

1. Beginning about a week before the meeting, contact the program participants and remind them of their assignments. These include:
   - Program chair who will contact speakers
   - President-elect who will ensure that the meeting is properly arranged
   - Committee chairs who will give reports at the meeting
   - Other functionaries

2. If any functionary or other participant is unable to fulfill an assigned role, ensure that you get their report to present at the chapter meeting or arrange for a substitute in advance, not at the meeting.

3. Ensure that the program chair has obtained the necessary information to properly introduce the speaker (biographical data, speech title and theme, etc.).

4. Plan your introductions carefully, and schedule the program so it does not run overtime.

At the Meeting

1. Make sure that all meeting functionaries and participants are prepared and are in attendance. Introduce past presidents, national officers, staff, invited guests, and visiting dignitaries.

2. Respect those in attendance. That is, begin on time and end on time. Don't wait for those arriving late. Rearrange the agenda to accommodate latecomers who have a role, but don't slow the meeting down because of them. Once you have begun, keep the meeting running on schedule. You have the authority to ask participants who have exhausted their allotted time to immediately conclude their portion of the program. This holds in particular for long-winded speakers who have been told of their allotted time constraints. It is your job to make the tough decisions. That is why you were elected.

3. Follow the procedure outlined below:
   - Offer a word of thanks to those in attendance.
   - Say a few words about the nature of the forthcoming program to warm up the audience. Discuss the theme of the meeting.
   - Explain the duties of the chapter officers as they are introduced (or let them explain), and introduce them at the proper times.
   - Introduce the program chair, the company he/she works for, and supply any other pertinent information.

- Remain standing until the program chair has taken position and recognized you, then take your seat. A nod or gesture of acknowledgment is sufficient to indicate a transfer of control.
- Have the program chair introduce the speaker and the topic by title and include a brief description. Make sure the program chair does *not* say, "Here's Joe Safety, our speaker for today." Have the program chair interview the speaker prior to the meeting. Get some personal details so that he/she can deliver a grand introduction. Another thing, *don't just read the bio*. How boring!
- At the end of the presentation, lead the applause and offer a brief word of appreciation. Your function is to bridge the gap between presentations, maintaining the interest of the audience.

4. At the conclusion of the program, briefly thank all speakers, attendees, and honored guests. Adjourn.

Speaker Evaluation Check Sheet

Have you had your share of speakers who were "yawners"? Are you tired of monotone data dumps that left your chapters half asleep and looking for an early exit? Well, one way to avoid a repeat performance is to have key people evaluate the speaker. It is good for historical purposes, as well as providing good feedback for the speaker. Here is an example evaluation check sheet.

1. Organization
    a. What's the point?
       - Why did the speaker wish to communicate (desire to motivate, convince, entertain, etc.)?
       - What idea or point was conveyed?
    b. Were you confused?
       - Was the purpose clearly understood from beginning to end?

– Did any part seem inappropriate for the topic; did you find yourself asking "So what?" or "How does this relate?"

2. Effectiveness
   a. Were there any distractions?
      – Any inappropriate mannerisms (jumping eyebrows, lip-smacking, ignoring part of the audience with eye contact)?
      – Any nervous habits (fidgeting with notes, pencils, clothes; "um's" or "ah's" or other repetitive phrases such as "you know" or "well")?
   b. What were the attractions?
      – Any effective visual techniques (hand or body gestures, visual aids, facial expressions)?
      – Any clever "twists" or other effective techniques (dramatic opening or ending; voice inflections; involvement of audience, such as a question and response interplay; etc.)?

3 Your personal reaction?
   a. How have you been affected?
      – Do you see the world differently?
      – How are you changed?

Perhaps these suggestions can help you run a more effective chapter meeting and influence members to look forward to next month. A well-run meeting indicates professionalism and may even elicit more member involvement. Maybe you can even cure some of the apathy we hear all too much about.

Robert's Rules

We have all been in meetings that were so long that our clothes went out of style. We have sat through more babblings and pontifications than any human should have to endure. One day I decided that I would fix that problem, so I bought a copy of *Robert's Rules of Order*. Upon reading this book, I discovered numerous tools that I could use to streamline the meetings. I learned things like:

1. Point of order! You are out of order!
2. If you didn't ask to add that to the agenda when I asked, it will not be considered.
3. We can't talk about that! It's already been discussed and voted on!
4. Point of order! You are out of order!
5. Mr. Chairman, I move that we call the question!
6. Point of order! You are out of order!
7. Call the question!
8. Point of order! You are out of order!

+ **Point of order.** What does point of order really mean? It means that some arcane rule of meeting conduct has been broken. Many people have no clue, so if you can influence them into thinking you know the rules and they don't, you can speed the meeting along. That was my goal! It also means, for instance, that you are talking about a specific item and they have interjected an unrelated item. See the meeting tips shown below.

+ **Agenda items.** When you start a meeting, ask if anyone who can vote would like to add items to the agenda. This is like marriage . . . speak now or forever hold your peace. If they want to add it later because they want to get preachy, forget it.

+ **Rehashing old business.** This is verboten, unless of course the whole group votes to reopen the issue. This is a good time to use the "point of order" phrase.

+ **Call the question.** This means, let's stop talking about this and vote on it. Most people do not understand that only the chair can call the question. Anyone can say "Call the question," but it must go to a vote, and a majority rule results in voting on the item on the floor. Without a majority it goes back to discussion.

What you must come to realize is that knowing Robert's rules of order gives you control because you have the knowledge and skills to speed meetings along unfettered by babblers and pontificators (see Figure 1). By merely knowing Robert's rules you can be perceived as smarter that the average bear and, interestingly, people will look to you for leadership. But there is more, much more, to leadership than this.

Leadership at Meetings

Essential qualities of a leader during meetings are as follows:

+ **An open mind.** Leaders are free thinkers, not influenced by strong vocal factions within the membership. An open mind toward problems and their solutions is a prerequisite for a leader.
+ **Creative thinking.** Leaders who are stuck with "doing it the way we have always done it" won't be very helpful in moving the organization forward. Leaders must be open to new ideas.
+ **Empathy.** Members will seek out the leader for consultation, advice, and support. Empathy for members' concerns and the ability to lend an understanding ear will serve the leader well.
+ **Enthusiasm.** There should be a genuine interest and enthusiasm for the goals of the organization, with the leader communicating that interest and enthusiasm to others.
+ **Good interpersonal skills.** The ability to get along with others, to be a part of the team effort, to give credit where credit is due, and to use strong leadership and diplomacy alternately as needed, is vital for a leader.

Action Desired	Motion	Sample Wording	Votes Required
Introduce business.	Main motion.	I move to donate $500 to the ASSEF.	Second & majority.
Change or modify a motion before adoption.	Amend.	I move to amend the motion by striking $500 and inserting $600.	Second & majority.
Have a few members study or take charge of a matter.	Commit or refer.	I move to refer the motion to a committee to be appointed by the chair to investigate and report with a recommendation at the next meeting.	Second & majority.
Postpone making a decision.	Postpone to a certain time.	I move to postpone consideration of this motion until after the adoption of the budget.	Second & majority.
Change rules of debate temporarily on this motion.	Limit or extend limits of debate.	I move that the debate be limited (or extended) to five minutes on this motion.	Second & 2/3 majority.
Stop debate and have a vote taken immediately.	Call the question.	Call the question of the pending motion or, I move to stop debate.	2/3 majority vote. No debate.
Set aside a matter to take care of an emergency.	Lay on the table.	I move to lay the pending motion on the table.	Second & majority. No debate.
Reopen consideration of a motion that has been tabled.	Take from the table.	I move to take from the table, the motion on the table regarding the $500 donation to the ASSEF.	Second & majority. No debate.
Protest about the noise, heating, ventilation, etc.	Question of privilege.	I rise to a question of privilege. May I open a window?	No second or debate. Chair decides.
Have a short intermission.	Recess.	I move to recess for 10 minutes. Or I move to recess until we obtain a quorum.	Second & majority. No debate.

Action Desired	Motion	Sample Wording	Votes Required
Close a meeting.	Adjourn.	I move to adjourn.	Second & majority. No Debate.
Set a time for continuation of the current meeting.	Fix the time to which to adjourn.	I move that when the meeting adjourns, it adjourn to meet again at 7 P.M. tomorrow.	Second & majority. No debate.
Verify a voice vote.	Division of the assembly.	Division. Or, I call for a division.	Second & majority.
Do something against the rules or take up a question out of proper order.	Suspend the rules.	I move to suspend the rules that prevent our completing action on this item before adjourning.	Second & majority. No Debate for standing rule; 2/3 for rule of order.
Allow members an opportunity to reverse an affirmative vote taken on a motion.	Rescind.	I move to rescind the vote adopted at the last meeting to donate $500 to the ASSEF.	Second & 2/3 majority with notice.
Allow members to take another look at a decision they made.	Reconsider.	Having voted on the prevailing side, I move to reconsider my vote on the motion to donate $500 to the ASSEF.	Second & majority.

Figure 1. Meeting tips from *Robert's Rules of Order*.

+ **Knowledge.** Leaders must have a thorough understanding of the organization, its members, operation, and the issues before it.

+ **Sound judgment.** Leaders must weigh the pros and cons of an argument carefully before reaching a decision. A good leader doesn't jump to conclusions or make quick decisions without sufficient information.

+ **Thick Skin.** No strong leader will be loved by all. Those who aspire to leadership roles must be able to deal with political pressure and take the heat for unpopular but necessary decisions, such as eliminating a program that has been unsuccessful.

+ **Vision.** Vision is the ability to subordinate individual interests for the good of the organization as a whole, and the ability to understand the long-term effects of decisions made.

Followership at Meetings

Complementing any leader are followers. Every successful leader realizes the importance of having good followers. The best leaders know that they, too, at times, need to follow: A good follower will:

+ **Anticipate.** A good follower anticipates the needs of others, the possibility of an alternative plan or procedure, ways to bring new ideas before the organization, and problems the leader may encounter along with ways to deal with them.

+ **Create.** A good follower is able to help the leader create and maintain an open climate for discussion. A good follower creates a place for his or her own special skills and talents within the framework of the organization.

+ **Evaluate.** A good follower evaluates and makes suggestions for changes and improvements. A good follower offers advice and constructive criticism when asked to do so. A good follower gives feedback to others in the organization.

+ **Listen.** A good follower listens attentively with interest and understanding to the leader and to others in the meeting. A good follower thinks about what is being said as others speak, asks questions to clarify what is being said, and gives feedback to let others know that he or she understands what was said.

+ **Observe.** A good follower observes the leader and others in the meeting. A good follower notes how others feel, how they interact with each other, how they respond (or don't respond) to the discussion.

+ **Participate.** A good follower participates. A good follower does not leave everything up to the leader. A good follower does not sit silently during a meeting and then later criticize what went on. A good follower is actively involved in solving the problem or performing the task at hand.

+ **Prepare.** A good follower is prepared. A good follower studies the goals, problems, plans, and facts well ahead of time and becomes familiar with any history that might influence the present situation or problem.

+ **Question.** A good follower asks questions. A good follower does not blindly follow the majority. A good follower does not take an opposite stand just for the sake of promoting an argument. A good follower upholds his or her own standards, values, and ideals, but not in a dictatorial way.

+ **Respond.** A good follower responds in an appropriate manner both verbally and nonverbally.

What the Minutes Should Contain

1. Date and place of the meeting.
2. What officers were present and/or their substitutes.

3. Whether the minutes of the previous meeting were approved or disapproved.
4. Highlights of committee reports.
5. A record of what is done, *not* what is said—no personal comments, complimentary or otherwise.
6. A record of *all* "motions" that were made or withdrawn, whether they passed or failed, and, if applicable, the vote.
7. The name of those making motions and seconds.
8. The time of adjournment.
9. Administrator's and secretary's signature.

Guest Speaker Protocol—for Educational Sessions

Where we as professionals often fail miserably is when we emcee meetings at conferences or special seminars. You are the toastmaster—act like it, maintain control of the meeting and keep it moving.

+ **Recognizing special attendees.** This includes your officers, past award recipients of the organization, past chairmen, past committee chairs, elected VIPs, and others Also, be the first to clap when you announce the individual (something we often overlook).

+ **Issuing awards.** Recognize contributors in front of their peers. This is probably the only recognition they may get. Think about how to give awards (e.g., certificates to all committee members, plaques to chairs, etc.). Don't just hand awards to people and say thanks. Again, start the clapping and get the momentum going.

+ **Introducing speakers.** Please don't just say, "Here's our speaker." Introduce him or her —that's your job. Make the speaker feel special. Try to interview each one beforehand; at a minimum, get a biography. Find out something personal like "Is he married?" or "Does she have children, and how many?" that you can use to make the speaker feel welcome.

+ **Scripting.** Generate a rough script that includes key points that you want to say and things you want to do. Check them off as you go, so you don't miss anything. Consider doing the same thing for your meetings. If you look and act in command of the situation, guess what? Colleagues will think you are a professional and who knows, maybe they will want to get more involved.

A Sample Meeting Agenda for Conducting Effective Meetings

Call to order. Begin promptly with one rap of the gavel. A quorum (majority) needs to be present. The chair states, "The meeting will come to order."

Opening ceremonies (*Optional*). The meeting can begin with an invocation and/or the "Pledge of Allegiance." Make certain that if there is a flag present, it is properly displayed.

Reading and approving the minutes. The chair states, "The secretary will read the minutes of the preceding meeting." The secretary reads the minutes. Minutes should be brief but accurate. The administrator asks, "Are there any corrections or additions to the minutes?" If there are none, the minutes are approved as read.

You may elect to forego this by someone motioning, "I move that we dispense with the reading of the minutes." If seconded and passed, the reading of the minutes may be dispensed with.

Recommendations to the organization. Any recommendations, motions, or other business is presented to the organization for deliberation.

Status reports. Status reports include all organization status reports and ad hoc committee reports.

Committee/task force reports. Any committees and or task forces will report at this time.

Unfinished business. The chair *does not ask for* unfinished business, but proceeds to the first item of unfinished business. The chair will have a record of unfinished business on the agenda that is presented for consideration at this time.

New business. Before new business can be acted upon, it must be presented to the group in the form of a motion, resolution, or recommendation, with appropriate second, when required.

Adjournment. The chair acts as follows: Questions and states, "Is there anything further to come before this organization? If not, I will entertain a motion to adjourn." The chair responds, "So moved" or "I move that we adjourn." Another voting member seconds the motion. A vote is taken. If it passes, the meeting is adjourned.

It's been said that meetings are where the minutes are kept and the hours are lost. Put hours back into your life; shorten your meetings so that you can get work done. I remember when I was in the airport traveling to Lubbock one time to visit my brother. The fellow sitting next to me asked me where I was going. I proudly said Lubbock, Texas. He retorted, "Yeah. I spent a week there one night." Don't let your meetings be thought of like this. Conduct your business and get on with life. Always remember *Robert's Rules*.

TEN COMMANDMENTS OF A MEETING ATTENDEE

I. Acknowledge People.
There is nothing like a cheerful greeting.

II. Smile at People.
It takes more effort to frown than to smile.

III. Call People by Name.
This takes some doing, but goes a long way toward making someone feel part of the success.

IV. Be Friendly and Helpful.
You must first be a friend to have a friend.

V. Be Genuinely Interested in People.
Believe it or not, there is something to like about everyone.

VI. Seek Out People.
Do not limit yourself to a few friends.

VII. Be Generous with Praise and Cautious with Criticism.
Praise in public. Criticize in private.

VIII. Consider Others' Feelings.
There are three sides to every controversy, yours, theirs, and the truth.

IX. Be Alert to Give Service.
We are in these positions to serve the members.

X. Maintain a Sense of Humor.
Safety is serious business, but we must always be able to laugh at ourselves and with others.

The next thing we will tackle is the use of technology, like computers and e-mail. A common trap we can easily fall into is believing that all technology is good. As a result, we overuse this technology. It can blind us to the point that we focus too much on technology and misplace our objectives. We can get trapped in this world; that can hinder our future advancement.

Odds and Ends

Collect Calls: Twenty Ways to Get Your Customers to Pay Up Fast

So, you consult on the side for a little extra cash. You look around and there isn't much cash. Why not? What would you get if you took all your overdue invoices and laid them end to end? Would it look like a paper trail that would stretch from El Paso to Port Arthur and give you a Texas-sized case of heartburn? Well, it doesn't have to be that way. We all love to help other companies out in a time of need, but we all hate asking for money. By carefully deploying some guerrilla collection techniques, starting today, you can turn those invoices into a virtual Texas-sized oil gusher of cash for your business on the side.

Collections 101: Background

Before plunging ahead, let's just take a minute to be sure we've covered the basics. This is essential to achieve a high success rate.

Be a Sport (On Your Mark). Your personal style has an impact on your success rate. Yeah, they owe you money, but being overly demanding won't earn you any points, much less cash. In fact, it may make them stall even more. Try to determine what motivates someone, communicate well, and work with people to get paid. Cultivate a friendly, responsive attitude that makes customers actually want to pay you, and you're on your way to success.

Get Organized (Get Set). Sometimes all it takes to collect an overdue invoice is asking for it. But you can't ask for it if you can't keep track of it. Your billing records and details of your invoice-related conversations with clients should be meticulously updated. If you're currently mired in the many-scraps-of-paper method of organization (like your IRS records), invest in some software, like, right now! Two good programs are Goldmine 4.0, and ACT! which tracks communications with customers, as well as many others.

Dial (Go). Now that you're organized, make that call, *before* the bill is due. Start building a relationship with your clients by phoning every few weeks to assure yourself they're satisfied with your products or services. Follow up promptly on any complaints. By the time the deadline arrives, you'll be able to issue the friendly reminder as an afterthought.

Collections 102: The Master Class, Call for Backup

Try to stay away from credit. You don't want to be a charter member of Collectors Anonymous. Try to get paid before the final product. In many cases you know they aren't going to like the final report, and may not want to pay you for an answer they don't like. Put a clause in the contract that you get paid on the delivery of the final draft report, not the approval of the final draft or final report. Then they can't disapprove your report and not pay you. They have to pay you whether they like the report or not.

Also schedule meetings to brief your status after you are scheduled to be paid. If they haven't paid by the day of the meeting, postpone the meeting until they pay you. This may seem like hardball, but—no check, no meeting.

If you *must* accept credit, use the credit application to your advantage. Credit applications give you a discreet way of finding out the name of each client's bank. If it gets ugly and you have to obtain a court judgment to collect a payment in the future, you'll be able to make a beeline to the bank account you're going to attach instead of wasting time and lawyers' fees trying to locate it. If you have to collect money from a judgment, find out when they pay their employees (i.e., on the first of the month, the first and the fifteenth, etc.). They may not have money in the bank at any other time than this. Make sure you show up to collect on the day they pay their employees. You can be sure they will have money in their accounts.

Cut 'em a break. It's easy to train your clients to pay you on time if you give them a cash incentive, or a disincentive against being late. Offer a price break if they mail their check by an early deadline. As an alternative, charge monthly interest or a late fee on overdue bills. To bypass the sticky banking regulations that come with charging interest, opt for a flat "rebilling fee" of $10 or $15 a month.

Drop 'em a card. If clients understand why you need their money, they may be more willing to pay quickly. Explain to the client that the outstanding invoice is keeping your accountant from closing out the books for the quarter. This may help you to get paid promptly.

When all else fails, outsource. If those 120-day-old bills are taking valuable time away from your business, don't feel guilty about sending them to a collection agency. You may be able to defray the cost by negotiating a volume discount. You can also try resolving stubborn problems in small claims court. You don't need a lawyer, just good records.

Consider reporting anyone who has written bad checks intentionally to your state attorney general's office. Since this is a crime, you may wind up with some free legal help.

A final note. Many people think of bill collecting as a hostile process. But, you're actually doing your delinquent clients a favor by forcing them to get their lives in order.

The Trouble with Technology: Think Computers Improve Productivity? Not Always

Computers are the ubiquitous, silent servants of the modern office. With people and computers working in tandem, the office is a more productive place, right? Well . . . not always. The world of computers has some good fairies, but there are gremlins as well. You want to look out for the gremlins so that you can avoid falling into technology traps.

Four of the most common misconceptions about computers in the workplace are:

1. **People can really focus on computer work.** Not really. A better way of putting it is that people can really focus on computers. For instance, you must submit an annual report (to your boss, a company, the government, etc.). Last year you got smart and computerized the report to make it easier to publish in subsequent years. But wait! You are no longer using the word-processing software and spreadsheets you used last year. You have to arduously convert all of the bits and pieces to generate a useful document. You end up focus-

ing more on the computer than the task. A rule to apply is, if it takes longer manually, do it by computer. But if it takes longer using the computer, keep doing it manually. There is also a sliding scale you can use based on urgency. If you need the information immediately, definitely do it manually. If you have time to think it through and computerize the information, you slide the scale closer to computerization.

Using computers should be transparent to the task. You should be thinking, "How can I do this job better?" What are the conceptual principles underlying this answer? Certainly *not*, "How do I get this computer to do what I want it to do?" Unfortunately, you usually end up doing the latter.

Also, when people are focusing on computers they are not necessarily focusing on computer work. A peek at some workers' screens can be revealing. The hands you see hammering the keyboard may not be nailing down that project you assigned them. They may be about to become a Starfleet Commander by killing a hundred more Klingons. The hand stealthily guiding a mouse may not be working on that pie chart you asked for. Computer users even have a euphemism for on-the-clock game-playing, its called, "mouse practice." Some computer games even come equipped with a "boss screen." This is an innocuous graph or summary sheet that pops up with the touch of a key to placate your probing eyes. For many computer-game players, the escape key means just that.

Further, computer solitaire has resurrected a game that might otherwise have gone the way of the hula hoop. Not too long ago, my company hired a temporary to handle a special task. Whenever I walked by, the phone was glued to her ear. I thought she was working feverishly on my task. I had high hopes. Alas, I was let down; her results were poor. This confused me until her co-workers explained to me that, while the phone had appeared to be surgically implanted in her ear, her attention was focused on (you guessed it!) computer solitaire.

It has been estimated that American businesses lose about $100 billion a year because of PC gaming. Ouch! So much for improved productivity! This rivals the obligatory coffee break. I know employees who have been reprimanded and even fired for playing games at work. We should all live by the opposite of Nike's slogan, "Just **don't** do it!"

2. **Electronic mail makes it easier for people in the office to stay in touch.** Unfortunately, sometimes the people who get in touch are the ones from whom you don't want to hear. Self-important memo writers or idle scribblers can clutter your e-mail with an endless parade of electronic debris. E-mail improves communication only if the people who receive it are the people who need to receive it. Otherwise, e-mail provokes a babble of opinions. Just read a few, you've got to agree.

I recently returned to my office from an out-of-town-conference. I had at least a hundred e-mail messages waiting for me. I spent five hours reading things like a list of the twenty-five shortest books, how to check my personality using colors, a Valentine's Day card executable file, and on and on and on.

3. **Computers can store a ton of information.** Yes, and your attic can store a ton of junk. You can squirrel away item after item in your computer memory. The problem is, will you ever be able to find it again? Probably not. Try to find an old tennis racket among the boxes of miscellaneous junk in your attic.

Even the most spacious attic can be overloaded. It's the same with computer memory. The more you can store, the more difficulty you have in storing. A computer has only so much brainpower, the more it uses for remembering, the less it has for thinking (running your software).

4. **Computers make people creative.** Not so. Computers are servants. Computers don't do what you want them to do; they do what you explicitly tell them to do. They don't teach creativity, although they do make it easier for some people to enhance their creative ideas. A graphics program, for example, can let you draw objects with perfect symmetry and revise your work easily.

    But computers also make noncreative, wasteful doodling more fun than ever. There are drawings beyond the dreams of madness, intellectual graffiti scrawled into the image files of many a computer.

    And computers can tempt even the uninspired into fits of "creation." A good example is the ability to format. I've read overformatted, pretentious prose that left me baffled. Add to this the ability to vary colors, and you can suffer seasickness as you try to read your e-mail.

A few words of advice:

+   **Purge game applications.** There's no nice way of saying it. Work time is for work. Having a card table and video arcade beckoning from a few feet away makes work seem like a world of dreariness.
+   **Tell your people that you don't want bulletin board e-mail sent to all and sundry.** Clean out the attic from time to time. You can do so by throwing out obvious junk. Delete it!
+   **Make sure the people in your office have the software they need to do their jobs, but beware of letting every-**

one have everything. Aspiring artists who weren't hired
to do artwork stay out of harm's way more easily if they
don't have an alluring graphics program.

Follow these rules and you'll cut down on workplace distractions. How many distractions do you think you can find in the
silicon-chip wonderland? You'd need a computer to figure it out!

All This Technology . . . But Where is the Productivity?

The Information Explosion

There has been more information produced in the last 30 years
than during the previous 5,000. A weekday edition of *The New
York Times* contains more information than the average person
was likely to come across in a lifetime in seventeenth-century
England. The information supply available to us doubles every
five years.

It used be said that technology advances redoubled every five
years. But that cycle has shortened to six months and continues
to shorten today. We've seen advances in processors, both speed
and size; advances in memory capability from megabytes to giga-
bytes and now terabytes; and a huge proliferation of computing
capability in the United States and worldwide. We have more
computer-related tools available to us than ever before. Tools that
can help us do our jobs more effectively than ever before. Tools
that can do the mundane tasks that we all dread. Many of these
tools are truly amazing.

Where Has All the Productivity Gone?

We can conservatively estimate that since 1980 the United States
has increased its aggregate computing power by a factor of something like 100 million. Yet worker productivity has grown slug-

gishly, only 1% annually. Compare this to the 1950s and 1960s when productivity grew 2–3 percent annually without all the computer power we have today. *How can that be?*

Some say bean counters never could estimate human productivity accurately. "Bean counters can only count beans, not flavor." Others suggest that it's basically a labor problem. You can't just dump smart machines on workers and expect them to know how to use them. You have to hire teachers to train them, which costs money, and companies don't want to do that, especially after spending a gazillion dollars to upgrade their computer systems. It's also a product of management's frustration from being badgered by employees begging for more technology, salespeople with graphs and charts illustrating the reasons technology can answer all their questions, followed by having to hire more people. Wait a minute—I thought buying these computers was going to keep me from hiring people!

Then there is the less charitable goof-off theory: Machines induce laziness. First machines took over the heavy lifting and our bodies got lazy. A disciplined few exercised and kept in shape. But the rest became couch potatoes. Computers have had the same effect on our minds. We work our gray matter less hard than we used to.

A pot-bellied driver of a bulldozer doesn't hurt productivity much because the bulldozer completely displaces human muscle. Computers however, depend on the human intellect. The computer is only as good as the person using it. A flabby mind can still suck the productivity gain right out of your company.

Then there's the usability of technology theory. Let's say you have this fancy dosimeter that takes all kinds of data on the noise being measured. We spend all of our time playing with the computer to figure out how to download the information from the instrument, because the user's manual doesn't begin to tell you how to do it. We finally get the information into a spreadsheet or our word-processing software only to realize we would have spent a fraction of the time writing down the exposure value from the LCD display and manually inputting it into the computer. This leads me to conclude that we may have gone too far in trying to computerize everything, or that the makers of this fancy software don't have a clue about how to make the software usable by people in the field. Perhaps this is one clue to why computer use hasn't increased productivity like many had hoped.

Much of the downsizing that has occurred in the last 10 years may reflect management's late recognition of this fact. To put it in the harshest possible terms, the productivity mistake of the 1980s may have been failing to move workers out as computers moved in. Old-guard managers woke up only after new competitors bought their machines and hired lean, mean, computer-smart workforces and began taking over the market.

What Does This Mean for "Net" Surfers?

It means "Don't spend all day dinking around on the Net!" Log on, get what you need, and log off, especially during working hours. After all, that's what our employers are paying us to do—a job—not to *have fun* surfing the Net all day. I generally set no more than four to five bookmarks and one to two list serves. That way I don't spend all day going through an endless parade of electronic debris that is more a hindrance than a help. As downsizing becomes more prominent, too much Net surfing could get you laid off. Use it as the information source and global e-mail network it was meant to be. Who knows, maybe we'll start to remember our family's names again.

What You Should—and Shouldn't—Say When You Send Those E-Mail Messages

Most e-mail users rarely forget to check the spelling in the messages they compose. But they often neglect to check how their communication will come across to their readers. Even well-meaning individuals write messages that they would never say aloud. To make sure your e-mail doesn't short-circuit a business relationship, consider these common-sense guidelines:

+ **Think about** who may read your message. You need to consider not only the person the message is for, but also anyone else who may read it. Consider the possibility that your message will take an unexpected electronic turn and appear in the wrong mailbox. Do you need to comment about a third party in your message? Is what you need to say negative or could it be construed as such? If so, consider using the phone or meeting in person instead.

+ **Try to** picture how your message's receiver will react when reading your message. Would you say to this person face to face the same thing you're writing? Have you inadvertently been sarcastic or judgmental? Is the receiver someone who's sure to put a negative spin on your message?
  Remember: If you were conversing orally, you might attempt to temper the bluntness in your message, or the exasperation you feel, with a grin or a teasing tone. But that's difficult to do with e-mail, even if you use a smile symbol. Why chance creating anxiety or even distrust by sending messages that lack human warmth?

+ **Avoid starting** a message by saying something like: "Why didn't you answer me sooner?" Some procrastinators may deserve this kind of blunt reminder, but you'll do more for the relationship if you open with a face-saving statement.

Example: "I wasn't sure if my message got through yesterday, so here it is again." Electronic messages that begin with "Why didn't you" come across as even more directing and authoritative than when you talk on the phone or in person.

+ **Ask yourself** whether you would be embarrassed if a member of your family read the message you plan to send. Why risk sending something that has innuendoes or remarks that would offend anyone. Apply what I call the "Aunt Alma test." If my proper and prissy Aunt Alma would not find the remark amusing or appropriate, I scrap it. You'll probably be better off if you save your funny remarks and jokes to use in a face-to-face conversation with an audience you know will be amused. At least then you'll have the opportunity to backpedal if you get a negative reaction.

+ **Make sure** your message is not too cryptic. Have you clearly and concisely said all the reader needs to know? Or have you withheld just enough of the details so that you retain control and force the reader to read between the lines, guess, or assume? *Keep this in mind*: Information control is a communication power play that can backfire very easily.

+ **Check your** messages for grammar idiosyncrasies. Have you fallen into the habit of using the ellipsis instead of completing your thoughts? Do you get carried away with peculiar punctuation—the e-mail symbols many writers use to take the place of words or to indicate thoughts and feelings? Some symbols may confuse instead of communicate.

+ **Reread and** then reread messages again before you send them. Would you be offended by the tone? If your tone is brusque, the receiver may think that he or she has done something to offend you. Or suppose you're the type who has trouble telling a joke; your reader may interpret your tone as satirical and as a cover for irritation and exasperation—which it very well might be.

+ **Do you** consistently write more than you need? Are you swamping your readers with too many unrelated and unnecessary details? Do you give so much information—important and unimportant and in no particular order—that your poor reader cannot easily conclude what matters and what doesn't?

Consider the results of a business poll reported in *Oregon Business*. The poll found that 26 percent of e-mail users spend an hour each day reading and responding to e-mail. And 14 percent spend more than an hour. So, do everything you can to compose messages that will help your readers save time. *Some guidelines*:

+ **Limit your** messages to one screen so receivers won't have to scroll up and down to grasp all that you've said.
+ **Use bullets,** numbers, underlining, boldface, and other optoins to highlight key points.
+ **Do you** clutter people's valuable electronic space with non-urgent items that you could fax or send by regular mail? Do you immediately broadcast every little tidbit you come across? Don't assume that those you communicate with aren't up to speed on the latest news and trends. Again, they may well think you're patronizing them by sending common-knowledge information.

  This also falls under the "know your audience" heading. As much as possible, you should make it your business to know what information sources they use regularly. If you know they subscribe to magazine X or online service Y, it makes no sense to fire off a message telling them about something you just read there.

+ **Don't let** e-mail become a substitute for in-person or phone conversations. Guard against using e-mail to converse with your colleagues in the offices next door. Unless the message must absolutely be in writing, try communicating the old-fashioned way: face to face. Walk down the hall or to the next building to speak with colleagues. Invite them to lunch. Or use the phone. Often, a phone conversation takes a fraction of the time needed to compose a message, send it, and wait for an answer.

+ **Keep in** mind that readers will respond more willingly to the writer who remembers the human element in communication. Do you think to add a personal line or two when you know the reader well? Do you remember to say thank you? The message medium may be cutting edge, but it will never replace the old-fashioned "thank you" and "please."

Until some clever person programs a courtesy checker, you'll profit from your own courtesy check. That means you must recognize that the tone of what you write should reflect the kinds of messages you expect to find in your electronic in-basket.

We have discussed the challenges of implementing safety, treating safety as a business function, leadership, conducting yourself in meetings, and carefully using technology. As we draw to a close, we will put a period on this discussion by answering the question, "Are You a Professional?"

Epilogue

Are You a Professional?

The term "professional" is routinely applied to doctors, or lawyers, or someone else who has gone to school for a long time, earned a number of degrees, and acquired a great deal of knowledge and technical know-how—gaining the title along with diplomas and status in society. In the business world, being a professional certainly does bestow status and advantage to those on the higher rungs of the magical corporate ladder. But we all know doctors and lawyers who are not very "professional" even though they are considered "professionals." Ironically, the aura surrounding the word has very little to do with the number of degrees that hang on the office wall.

I think being a professional means being thorough. It means doing research and following through. It means being responsible and accountable for every aspect of a job from beginning to end and performing proficiently and with competence. It also means knowing the "rules of the game."

So, even though the office hours are eight to five, if your boss arrives at 7:30 A.M., are you expected to be there? Even though the president of the company says he has an "open door" policy, what is the actual protocol? Is it okay to be autonomous? What are the limits of what you can do autonomously? What scores a point with your boss, the president? Answer these questions and you're defining some of the rules of the game.

But *knowing* the rules of the game isn't sufficient, you must also know how to *play* the game. It is like the difference between knowledge and wisdom. Knowledge is knowing the facts of a particular discipline, whereas wisdom is applying this knowledge to life. You need to know how to *play* the game.

A professional is creative and eager to learn how to play the game in the best possible way. That means playing so that both you and the company win. Professionals know how to compete successfully, and how to be successful team members, all within the rules of the game.

Another rule of the game is exercising discretion. Being professional means not putting yourself, your boss, or your company in any kind of jeopardy by betraying trust. A professional adheres to the strictest code of ethics, fair play, integrity, cooperation, and confidentiality.

If a condition exists in your office, or something comes to your attention, that you believe is unethical or improper, and you are unable to rectify the situation, you may even have to leave the job. Endless discussion in the rest rooms, head shaking, and jaw flapping will serve neither you nor the company to any good purpose.

Professionalism also develops as an outgrowth of ambition and experience. The person who sets goals and strives for status, power, or position finds that assuming and assimilating the attributes and attitudes of the professional provides a better route to advancement than anything else.

Some of the attributes of a professional are:

+ **Being responsible, efficient, and resourceful.** You must have an inner sense of commitment to your work. You must support the objectives of your organization. You must give your job top priority during working hours. You must meet deadlines and follow through to complete projects.

+ **Being flexible and cooperative.** You must set aside problems while at work. You must be able to receive direction without getting defensive. You must adhere to the standards of dress and demeanor. You must be able to shift mental gears to meet unexpected needs. You must help where needed even when it is outside your specific job description.

+ **Being wise, objective, and sensible.** You must evaluate your work realistically and objectively. You must set your goals to be compatible with the organization's. You must know when to speak and when to be silent. You must know when to accept the judgment of your boss and when to disagree. You must judge others by their competence, not their personalities.

So, there you have it—my advice for thinking, and getting, "Out of the Box." If you are looking to transition your career or survive a merger, perhaps this book will assist you in achieving your goal. With the inevitable and continuous change in the business world today, I hope this book will help you manage your career successfully and avoid those career-destroying land mines. *Best Wishes, from one battle-scarred professional to another.*

Bibliography

Allison, William W. *Profitable Risk Control*. Des Plaines, IL: American Society of Safety Engineers, 1986.

American Institute of Chemical Engineers. *Guidelines for Hazardous Evaluation Procedures*, 2nd ed. New York: AICE, 1992.

_____. *Guidelines for Technical Management of Chemical Process Safety*. Center for Chemical Process Safety (CCPS), New York: AICE, 1989.

American Petroleum Association. *Management of Process Hazards, API Recommended Practice 750*, 1st ed. Washington, DC: APA, January 1990.

Bajarin, Tim. "Taking Future Stock." *Houston Computer Currents*, (June 1996): 8.

Bird, Frank E. and George E. Germain. *Practical Loss Control Leadership*. Atlanta, GA: Institute of Publishing, 1990.

Brauer, Roger L. *Directory of Computer Resources*. Des Plaines, IL: American Society of Safety Engineers, 1994.

Brigham, Eugene F. *Fundamentals of Financial Management*. Chicago, IL: Dryden Press, 1989.

DeHart, R. E. and E. J. Gremillion. "Process Safety—A New Culture." Paper presented at the Occupational Safety & Health Summit, February 1992.

Department of Defense Military Standard. MIL-STD-882C, *System Safety Program Requirements*. Washington, DC: Department of Defense, February 1993.

English, William. *Strategies for Effective Workers' Compensation Cost Control*. Des Plaines, IL: American Society of Safety Engineers, 1988.

Grant, Eugene L. and Lawrence F. Bell. *Basic Accounting and Cost Accounting*. New York: McGraw-Hill, 1964.

Hansen, Mark D. "The Safety Professional's Survival Guide," American Society of Safety Engineers, Proceedings of the Annual Professional Development Conference & Exposition, Orlando, Florida, June 25–28, 2000.

_____. "After the Cherry Picking." *Industrial Safety & Hygiene News* (May 1998): 17–18.

_____. "Business Sense for Engineers." *Plant Services* (September 1998): 112–114.

_____. "Do You Lead or Manage?" *Industrial Safety & Hygiene News* (February 1997): 24–25.

_____. "Environmental Safety & Health Compliance in the 1990's." *Professional Safety* (February 1994).

_____. "Fire-proofing Your Job." *Industrial Safety & Hygiene News* (February 1998): 18.

_____. "First, Pay Your Dues." *Industrial Safety & Hygiene News* (September 1998): 16.

_____. "How Do You Know Where Safety Fits In? All About Assessing Corporate Cultures." *Industrial Safety & Hygiene News* (October 1997): 26–27.

_____. "You Have to Talk Dollars and Cents (Part 3)." *Industrial Safety & Hygiene News* (July 1997): 20.

Hansen, Mark D., Richard M. Harley, and Henry W. Grotewold. "Dollars and Sense: Using Financial Principles in the Safety Profession." *Professional Safety* (June 1997): 36–40.

Hawks, J. L. and J. L. Mirian. "Create a Good PSM System." *Hydrocarbon Processing* (August 1991).

International Organization for Standardization. *ISO 9001: Quality Systems - Model for Assurance in Design/Development, Production, Installation and Servicing.* London: ISO, 2000.

_____. *ISO 9002: Quality Systems—Model for Assurance in Production and Installation.* London: ISO, 2000.

_____. *ISO 9003: Quality Systems—Model for Assurance Final Inspection and Test.* London: ISO, 2000.

_____. *ISO 9004: Quality Management and Quality System Elements—Guidelines.* London: ISO, 2000.

Kletz, T. *What Went Wrong? Case Histories of Process Plant Disasters,* 3rd ed. Houston: Gulf Publishing Company, 1994.

Krembs, J. A. and James M. Connolly. "Analysis of Large Property Losses in the Hydrocarbon & Chemical Industries." Paper presented at the 1990 NPRA Refinery and Petrochemical Plant Maintenance Conference, San Anotonio, Texas, May 23–25, 1990.

Lees, F. P. *Loss Prevention in the Process Industries.* London: Butterworths, 1980.

Malloy, Rich. "Say Goodbye to Windows 3.1." *Mobile Office* (April 1995): 49–50.

MacKenzie, Alec. *The Time Trap: The Classic Book on Time Management*, 3rd ed. New York: AMACOM, 1997.

Nikolai, Loren A. and John D. Bazley. *Intermediate Accounting.* Boston, MA: PWS-Kent Publishing, 1988.

O'Lone, E. J. "Datapro, Document Imaging Systems, Management Issues." *Client/Server Computing* (June 1993): 1–8.

Pargh, Andy. "Gadget Guru's Guide to Buying a Computer." *USA Today*, 19 August 1996.

Powell, James A. "Buyer Beware." *Windows Magazine* (April 1996): 32.

Riggs, James L. *Production System: Planning, Analysis and Control.* Wiley/Hamilton Series in Management and Administration. New York: Wiley, 1976.

Silverman, D. "Latest Presarios Boast Speed, Accessories." *Houston Chronicle*, 4 February 1996.

Tarquin, Anthony J. and Leland T. Blank. *Engineering Economy.* New York: McGraw-Hill, 1976.

Theland, David S. "Management of the Work Environment." *Selected Safety & Health Readings*, vol. III, Project Minerva. Washington, DC: U.S. Department of Health and Human Services, 1988.

Turner, Wayne C., J. H. Mize, and Kenneth E. Case. *Introduction to Industrial and Systems Engineering.* Englewood Cliffs, NJ: Prentice-Hall, 1987.

Watts, James P. and Mark L. Ruder. *Certified Safety Professional Home Study Workbook.* Las Vegas Safety Workshops, 1992.